Politeness and Poetry
in the Age of Pope

Politeness and Poetry in the Age of Pope

Thomas Woodman

Rutherford ● Madison ● Teaneck
Fairleigh Dickinson University Press
London and Toronto: Associated University Presses

Associated University Presses
440 Forsgate Drive
Cranbury, NJ 08512

Associated University Presses
25 Sicilian Avenue
London WC1A 2QH, England

Associated University Presses
P.O. Box 488, Port Credit
Mississauga, Ontario
Canada L5G 4M2

The paper used in this publication meets the requirements of the American National Standard for Permanence of Paper for Printed Library Materials Z39.48-1984.

Library of Congress Cataloging-in-Publication Data

Woodman, Thomas, 1945–
    Politeness and poetry in the age of Pope / Thomas Woodman.
     p.cm.
    Bibliography: p.
    Includes index.
    ISBN 0-8386-3348-X (alk. paper)
    1. English poetry—18th century—History and criticism.
    2. Courtesy in literature.   3. Pope, Alexander, 1688–1744-
    -Contemporary Great Britain.   4. Etiquette—Great Britain-
    -History—18th century.   I. Title.
    PR555.C687W66   1989
    821'.5'09353—dc19   88-45806
                                                                         CIP

PRINTED IN THE UNITED STATES OF AMERICA

Contents

Preface

A comprehensive account of the matter of politeness in eighteenth-century Britain is needed today. This book does not
purport to offer such an account, though it briefly surveys the
terrain. It began instead as an investigation into the work of
Alexander Pope and a small group of his friends and associates.
It became clear that all of them, like many other writers of the
period, were deeply concerned with questions of politeness but
that Pope alone sought to preserve in its fullness the Renaissance
poet's traditional responsibility "to form the manners."

Many people have helped in various ways with this project. I
owe thanks, for example, to Stephen Copley, Brean Hammond
and Nigel Wood. My colleagues Patrick Parrinder, Ron Knowles,
Cedric Brown and Carolyn Lyle have read and commented on
sections. Thomas Yoseloff of Associated University Presses has
always been very helpful. I want also to give especial thanks to
my parents and my wife Rosemary.

I am grateful for permission to recast brief extracts of my
previous works, *Thomas Parnell* (copyright © 1985) to G. K. Hall
& Co., Boston; "Pope and the Polite" (January 1978) and "Parnell,
Politeness and Pre-Romanticism," (July 1983) to the editor of
Essays in Criticism; and " 'Vulgar Circumstance' and 'Due Civil-
ities:' Gay's Art of Polite Living in Town," in *John Gay and the
Scriblerians* (London: Vision Press, 1988; New York: St. Martin's
Press, 1989) to Vision Press.

I am also grateful to the Oxford University Press for permission
to quote from *Swift Poetical Works*, edited by Herbert Davis
(1967); *Matthew Prior: Literary Works*, edited by H. Bunker
Wright and Monroe K. Spears (1959); and *John Gay, Poetry and
Prose*, edited by Vincent A. Dearing and Charles E. Beckwith
(1974); to Methuen and Co., for permission to quote from *The
Poems of Alexander Pope*, edited by John Butt (1963); and to the
University of Delaware Press for permission to quote from *Col-
lected Poems of Thomas Parnell*, edited by Claude Rawson and F.
P. Lock (1989).

Politeness and Poetry
in the Age of Pope

Introduction

The idea that the eighteenth century was somehow a peculiarly polite and elegant age in England will hardly survive a look at the evidence. In J. H. Plumb's well-known words, "The Age of Walpole was rough, coarse, brutal; a world for the muscular and the aggressive and the cunning."[1] An emphasis on the "Age of Refinement" has always consorted oddly with the images of gin-shops and crime—the sights, sounds, and smells of eighteenth-century London presented, for example, in Hogarth, Fielding, and Smollett. Today it is these latter implications that historians and critics are more likely to explore, though there has been a small shift of emphasis again in recent work on aristocratic domination in the period and in J. C. D. Clark's view of England as an "ancien régime."[2]

The great interest in politeness in the period is certainly undeniable. James Miller, writing in 1738, complained that it had become the "Coxcomb's Av'rice, Courtier's Claim / The Citt's Ambition and the Soldier's Fame" (*Of Politeness*, London, 3–4). It would be wrong to underestimate the considerable social and cultural achievements that the period included under the umbrella term of politeness. It would be equally wrong to deny that the interest had an anxious and paradoxical side, or that politeness often had to define itself against its opposite.

As the structuralists have made plain, there is no human state of nature prior to culture and society, and all societies are constituted out of codes and conventions. It would be doctrinaire and simplistic to try to explain all this vast complex of traditional social behavior in terms of different ruling classes justifying and enforcing their position. Yet links with power structures can hardly be denied either. The instinct to portray as natural and unquestionable what in fact serves the interests of an elite is a widespread one.[3] It goes far beyond simple propaganda on the part of a ruling class, though it can obviously include that.

A time-honored system develops, with unconscious as well as conscious elements, a widely accepted, almost unchallengeable way of explaining the status quo. The ancient sense of manners

as customary behavior, both social and moral, implies an un-
changing and hierarchical social order in which each grouping
has a preordained and fitting way to behave.

It would be hard therefore, to deny that manners have a powerful *ideological* dimension, if that problematic but indispensable
word is taken in the general sense as referring to "those modes of
feeling, valuing, perceiving and believing" that have "a relation
to the maintenance and reproduction of social power."[4] Pierre
Bourdieu puts it more strongly:

> All societies . . . that seek to produce a new man through a process of
> "deculturation" and "reculturation" set . . . store on the seemingly
> most insignificant details of *dress, bearing* physical and verbal *man-
> ners*. . . . The whole trick of pedagogic reason lies precisely in the
> way it extorts the essential while seeming to demand the insignifi-
> cant . . . the concessions of *politeness* always contain *political* con-
> cessions.[5]

Even at the most superficial level attention to manners can be
used to indicate leisure, prosperity and status.[6] Manners differentiate one class from another, marking social station. They
also provide guidelines for the necessary social interactions.
Manners oil the wheels of society. Recognition of their ideological dimension does not undermine their positive achievements,
even their necessity. They improve the quality of life by inculcat-
ing self-restraint and thus fostering what has been called the
"civilising process."[7] They soften the extremes of upper-class
domination and of male behavior toward women. But they rein-
force preconceived roles at the same time, masking class and
gender relations as well as revealing them and turning domination into gracious condescension. They define, control, and exclude.

The older mainstream traditions of manners are very specific
in providing a quasi-philosophical justification of the fitness of
an aristocracy or an elite to rule. Our social "betters" are presented as our moral betters as well. Aristotle wrote that "the more
nobly born are more fully citizens than the non-noble, good birth
being held in esteem in every country; and the offspring of the
better sort are likely to be better men, for good birth is excellence
of stock." The Greco-Roman tradition of civility presupposes
leisure and independent wealth as the necessary conditions for
engagement in civic affairs, and it is similarly only those with
the opportunity of contemplative leisure who can attain to the
virtue of the philosopher.[8] By the use of words like "noble" and

"gentle" medieval theory implies that high birth, good morals, and good manners are organically linked. "Gentle" and its many cognates obviously include the idea of *Gens*, stock.[9]

The normative connection between morals and gentle birth is potentially double-edged. It had to be conceded, of course, that not all the gentle of birth were gentle morally, nor all the ungentle of birth lacking in moral gentleness. When the Church put its authority behind chivalry it was attempting to reform aristocratic manners as well as providing a justification for them. As time went on, elements of resistance to the established norms could develop among the dispossessed or the highly intelligent even in the most traditional of societies. The moral code can theoretically be turned against the establishment as well as authorizing it, and the Stoic claim that virtue is the only true nobility is often echoed. This was strengthened by Christian ideals of poverty and humility, for " . . . hye God sometyme senden kan / His grace into a little oxes stalle." Had not St. Paul written to the Corinthians, "Take yourselves, brothers, at the time when you were called: how many of you were wise in the ordinary sense of the word, how many were influential people, or came from noble families?"[10]

The system had the great weight of the rich and powerful behind it, however, and it was complex enough in itself to cushion the effect of such recognitions and even incorporate them. Without exaggerating the uniformity of the Middle Ages or minimizing elements of resistance the pervasive influence of an ideal, almost archetypal set of norms can be discerned. The beautiful fiction of *Sir Gawain and the Green Knight*, for example, is obviously in part contrived to demonstrate that the smallest details of etiquette involve issues of social status, ethics, and religion. This is a system that no one fully articulates since, as soon as it is expressed, exceptions to it become obvious. Yet, precisely because the system is ideological and does not have to be believed literally in all its details, it is impossible to falsify it.

Even those systems of manners that seem to argue for a new democracy often end up justifying a new elite. The idea of learning as the only true gentility was strong in the early Renaissance, but the debate really becomes the focus for the struggles and then the accommodations between an older aristocracy and a newer elite of intellectuals and bureaucrats. Renaissance courtesy is given its own mystique in Neoplatonic terms, for in Castiglione the courtier's grace is seen by one speaker as the "gift of nature and of the heavens" rather than the product of human effort.[11]

Spenser's Tristram in book 6 of *The Fairie Queene* is similarly courteous in his very essence despite his upbringing in the forest.

The question of whether good manners are to be seen as "natural" or the product of education, full of social and political implications as it is, often calls up the whole elaborate philosophical complex of the art-and-nature debate. This may in turn take the form of an argument about town and country life. The superficial and unnatural life of the town can be contrasted with the plain living of the country, or the social climbing of the former set against the settled hierarchy of the latter. On the other hand a society can be thought of in terms of an Aristotelian art that fulfils nature, so that civility as a part of civic life is essentially urban. The criteria used to distinguish natural manners or manners that fulfil nature from unnatural and superficial ones usually, of course, involve contrasting the interests of an older ruling class with new elements that appear to threaten its status.

Johnson gives as sense 9 of "manners" the traditional meaning, mores, "General way of life, morals; habits," but he also gives as sense 10 the more modern sense of "ceremonious behaviour; studied civility." This certainly reflects some of that general demystification of convention throughout the Renaissance period that Lawrence Manley has described.[12] It is not a distinction that would have occurred to a more purely customary society, where the second sense would have been subsumed entirely under the first. The importance of etymology must not be exaggerated, but there is clearly some significance in the fact that usages involving the idea of "polish" or politeness become more prevalent in French and English during the late seventeenth and the eighteenth centuries.[13] A vast and complex series of social changes involving shifts of power, a degree of secularization, and the rise of commerce and capitalism necessitated ideological revisions. Manners as the fixed mores of a stratified society and "Courtesy," which as Spenser says, is "of Court," (*The Fairie Queene*, bk. 6, canto 1, stanza 1) modulate into politeness. For "politeness," as J. G. A. Pocock and others have shown, tends especially to be associated with the relatively flexible norms and exchanges of a commercial society.[14] Politeness also relates to the new sense of a "public space" set off from the direct activities of the state.

Such a development has been called "bourgeois," but as we shall see it is perhaps more appropriately regarded as an extension of the "cultural hegemony" of a more traditional upper class prepared to admit bourgeois elements, but only to a very limited degree.[15] Though the growth of commerce and consumerism in the eighteenth century enabled some interest groups to aspire to politeness for the first time, the great focus on manners primarily reflects the continuing upper-class process of definition, control, and exclusion.

Nevertheless, older traditions that are more obviously hierarchical need to be reinterpreted, and the aristocratic privileging of leisure becomes problematic in an age with a more direct sense of the importance of labor. The very metaphor of polish suggests ideological shifts. It raises the question of art versus artifice, since it stresses the nurture rather than the nature side of the great debate. It thus reflects the position of an elite that is no longer primarily differentiated by birth, whatever its aristocratic elements. The metaphor also unavoidably seems to imply an attention to surfaces—one thinks of Dickens's socialites, the Veneerings perhaps—and the usage often incorporates anxieties and reservations as well as positive senses. Even today the word carries more frigid connotations than that "courtesy" in which Yeats would like his daughter to be "chiefly learned" ("Prayer for my Daughter"). It does not retain Christian resonances or glamorous courtly connotations. William Empson comments aptly that all politeness has an element of irony about it.[16]

In the ancient ideal of decorum a link between literature and manners has always been recognized. Since, as a Restoration commentator put it, "Writing is a sort of conversing," it has to be governed by a similar etiquette.[17] The earliest metaphorical uses of the word "polish" refer to the arts rather than to social behavior, but the extension is a natural one, reflecting an obvious overlap between the fine arts and wealth, leisure, education, and social position. Eighteenth-century literature, though it certainly cannot be complacently characterized as polite in an unproblematic sense, reflects social interests and aspirations, and poetry in particular has a markedly upper-class bias in the first decades of the century. Sir Richard Steele, asked what was the main qualification for a poet, replied astonishingly," To be a very well-bred Man" (*Spectator*, No. 314). Certain revisions are also necessary, however, and significant debates about different models occur, like the argument about whether Dorimant in *The Man of Mode*[18] is really a fine gentleman or not. The conventional relationship between the poet and manners thus becomes a very relevant one for the period, particularly for that group of poets—

Parnell, Prior, Gay, Swift, and Pope—who are the central focus of this study. They have a strong sense of their conservative ideological responsibility to write on mores, but their sense of these traditions in changing circumstances is inevitably a diminished one. On the other hand they are profoundly ambivalent in their very traditionalism about certain aspects of the new politeness.

1

The "Courtier's Claim and the Citt's Ambition": Eighteenth-Century Versions of Politeness

Politeness, Consolidation, and Exclusion

To talk about "class" in eighteenth-century England is to enter naively into a theoretical minefield. Eighteenth-century writers did not themselves use the term, of course, preferring words like "rank," "estate," or "condition." Modern historians, divided partly but not exclusively along Marxist versus non-Marxist lines, have debated the appropriateness of using the word "class" itself as well as words like "bourgeois."[1] What does seem clear is that the power and prestige of the landed aristocracy remained very considerable during the eighteenth century. This was an age, as Lawrence Stone, John Cannon, and J. C. D. Clark have amply shown, of domination of the political system by elaborate aristocratic patronage and the reaffirmation and extension of the aristocracy's "cultural hegemony." It was natural enough for them to assert their status by an attention to decorum and conspicuous refinement of lifestyle. But the force of this assertion also reflected the memory of the mid-seventeenth-century traumas and concealed ideological anxiety and revision. To a considerable degree, as Michael McKeon has stressed, capitalist values are transforming this aristocracy, "eating away, as it were from within, at a social structure whose external shell still seems roughly assimilable to the status model."[2]

Politeness had also for some considerable time extended beyond the court and aristocracy. The steady expansion and growing prosperity of a wider elite is, as Lawrence Stone has shown, one of the most marked social developments of the whole Tudor period. If the aristocracy and the greater landed gentry had the central power, wealth, and status, this wider elite is still appropriately termed upper-class in a broader sense. Interest in education, the arts, polish, and fashion was the index of its growth. The number of graduates from the universities and the inns of court increased steadily before the civil wars. From Elizabeth's reign onward the gentry had taken seats in the House of Commons. The elite gradually came to include increasing numbers of bureaucrats and lawyers and upper gentry with no direct connection to the court.[3]

Sir Thomas Smith explained in 1612:

> For whosoever studieth the lawes of the realme, who studieth in the universities, who professeth liberall sciences, and to be shorte, who can live idly and without manuall labour, and will bear the port, charge and countenaunce of a gentleman he shall be called master, for that is the title which men give to esquires and other gentlemen, and shall be taken for a gentleman.[4]

This growth in the upper classes involved the gradual extension of what Norbert Elias has called "the civilising process," the spread of self-restraint and polite inhibitions as a means of indicating social respect for others. The increased educational opportunities, the huge growth of London, the development of "the season," the improvement in communications through private coaches and public carriers, and the popularity of foreign travel all helped to accelerate the interest in fashion, the arts, and "polish."

Attention to politeness was even more marked after the Restoration, as V. B. Heltzel has demonstrated.[5] The traditional aristocracy reasserted their position in this way, while the growth and cultural development of a broader upper class bore fruit especially now that the worst of the political conflicts had ended. Consumerism and an interest in fashion also accompanied the steady growth of a commercial society. The movement toward agrarian capitalism, the trade boom, the increase in investment, the national successes against France, and the proud, Whiggish sense of liberty after the Glorious Revolution strengthened the self-confidence of the whole oligarchy. Politeness, a matter of the arts as much as of behavior, reflects the positive cultural energy celebrated by Shaftesbury, who wrote that "the Figure we are likely to make Abroad and the Increase of Knowledge, Industry, and Sense at Home will render united *Britain* the Principal Seat of Arts." Leonard Welsted similarly hymned Liberty as giving "Politeness to Peace," and he is clearly using "politeness" as a general term for cultural health. The national temperament, politics, and trading opportunities have conspired to create a new state of polished perfection even in the English language, which is now freed from barbarism, refined and chaste in diction.[6] English Palladianism, with its combination of restraint and refinement, is obviously an analogous development in architecture.

London was described in 1741 as a "city famous for wealth, commerce and plenty, and for every other kind of civility and politeness."[7] From the Restoration on it grew at an enormous rate, and its cultural self-consciousness was increased by the rebuilding after the Great Fire. It became remarkable for what seemed like an explosion of prosperity and fashion. The great increase in the number of coaches led to traffic jams. The wealthier country gentry spent time in London every year, and the commercial boom made available a range of safe *rentier* incomes free from the obvious marks of trade and thus created the phenomenon of the so-called "pseudo-gentry" of the towns. The new prosperity and the social conditions of London accelerated the assimilation of the financiers, the greater merchants, the better-educated professional men and the "pseudo-gentry" into the "politer Part of Mankind." Shaftesbury described the process approvingly:

> All politeness is owing to liberty. We polish one another, and rub off our corners and rough sides by a sort of amicable collision.[8]

The increase in the prosperity and leisure opportunities of the urban "men of a middle condition"—tradesmen, bookkeepers, lesser merchants, and clerical workers—is also very marked. Moll Flanders looked for a tradesman as a husband "that was something of a Gentleman too; that when my Husband had a mind to carry me to the Court or to the Play, he might become a Sword, and look as like a Gentleman, as any other Man." Voltaire, observing the ordinary London populace in Greenwich Park, thought at first they must be the nobility because of their fashionable dress.[9] Politeness was bound to be a concern with London tradesmen, whose upper-class customers were so important to them. Jebediah Strutt sent his son a copy of Chesterfield's letters and stressed that "it is almost as necessary to learn a genteel behaviour, & polite manner, as it is to learn to speak, or read, or write."[10]

Considerable concern was expressed in the period about these symptoms of what one writer called the *"Genteel Mania"* and "imitating every station above our own." To the landed interest, especially the minor gentry, it was particulary threatening, and Bolingbroke exploited this, blaming it all on capitalism, and complaining that the "meanest grubs on earth have raised themselves by stock-jobbing to the rank and port of noblemen and gentlemen."[11] None of this really amounts to a rise of the middle classes as such, however. Obviously no coherent middle class in modern terms even existed in the period, and, despite the growing influence of what may appropriately be considered bourgeois values, the power of the actual urban bourgeoisie was very limited. The so-called "Genteel Mania" was a relatively superficial consequence of the new consumerism and represented no threat to the oligarchy. The backbone of English society remained an essentially rural order, though agrarian capitalism led to increasing involvement with city finance and town life was more and more the centre of the fashionable world. England continued to be governed by a "broad based but relatively closed oligarchy, part landed, part monied, under the leadership of a still narrower elite of extremely wealthy and influential landowners."[12] This oligarchy was itself implicated in the growth of a capitalist society by investment, borrowing, and consumerism, and its members were the chief beneficiaries.

Certain revisions of ideology were, nevertheless, required. The period saw a broader-based more superficial upper-class stylishness, much influenced by French traditions of the honnête homme.[13] Continuing and developing ideas like those of Sir Thomas Smith and others, Guy Miege says that "the title of Gentleman is commonly given to all that distinguish themselves from the common sort of people by genteel dress and carriage, good education, learning or an independent station." Lord Chesterfield is surprisingly dismissive of the importance of birth and says that even a ploughman can learn the graces.[14] Social "grace" in the eighteenth century has lost the quasi-religious element still apparent in Castiglione. It has become a more purely social quality, cut free from any transcendent dimension, yet at the same time heavily valued and mystified, "for that is most courtly and hardest to be imitated which consists of a Natural easiness and unaffected Grace, where nothing seems to be studied, yet everything is extraordinary." Dudley Ryder revealingly comments, "I don't find among these fine folks that their conversation is better or more improving than others or diverting than others, only they have a certain genteel manner of carrying it and saying very ordinary things without concern."[15]

The growth of London and the changes in the court after the Restoration and the 1688 revolution encouraged a movement away from elaborate ceremony, amusingly described in Addison's essay on manners in town and country. He says that:

Conversation, like the *Romish* Religion, was so encumbered with Show and Ceremony, that it stood in need of a Reformation to retrench its Superfluities, and restore it to its natural good Sense and Beauty. At present therefore an unconstrained Carriage, and a certain Openness of Behaviour are the height of Good breeding. The Fashionable World is grown free and easie; our Manners, sit more loose upon us: Nothing is so modish as an agreeable Negligence. In a word, Good Breeding shows it self most, where to an ordinary Eye it appears the least.

Unfortunately the country has not yet caught up, and

A Polite Country squire shall make you as many Bows in half an Hour, as would serve a Courtier for a week. There is infinitely more to do about Place and Precedency in a Meeting of Justices Wives, than in an Assembly of Dutchesses.[16]

Clearly in London and other towns a new sense of social freedom is developing. Epitomised in the popular institution of the coffee-house, it involves a public space set off from the organs of the state and the restrictions of court life. "The new coffee-house," write Peter Stallybrass and Allon White,

provided a mediation between domestic privacy and the grand public institutions of business and the state. At the same time whilst it stoutly and successfully resisted the interventions and interference of the State, it was an important instrument in the regulation of the body, manners and morals of its clientele in the public sphere. . . . It simultaneously undermined feudal rules of social hierarchy and precedence whilst extending within its relatively heterogeneous public the laws of decency and civility which Norbert Elias has rightly seen as playing an important role in the symbolic establishment of power.[17]

It seems an oversimplification, however, to call this new development "bourgeois." Mr. Wilson in *Joseph Andrews* is perhaps unduly rigorist when he talks of those "just without the polite Circles, I mean the lower Class of the Gentry, and the higher of the mercantile World." But if the most fashionable and influential of the merchants were in practice usually found acceptable, they cannot be taken as standing for the bourgeoisie as such. The conditions are laid down entirely from above. The new public sphere is the place for the *internalization* of controls. As John Cannon has argued, the "affirmation of the liberal and open nature of English society" was actually "one of the most potent ways by which the aristocracy reinforced its privileged position." Politeness thus represents the modification of traditional aristocratic attitudes and the co-opting of a wider polite elite through subtle instructions in such values. It proposes consensus, but it is in fact a narrow consensus in which the constraints are merely concealed. Politeness is ultimately a way of reconciling an aristocratic ethos with a limited acceptance of the aspirations of other classes in a laissez-faire economic system.[18]

It would therefore be a grave mistake to regard the relative relaxation of the sanctions of birth and protocol as genuinely democratic developments. The very need to redraw the ideological definitions of status meant a stronger need to eliminate what was not polite. The firm sense of exclusiveness between the polite and the rest was if anything deepened by the fact that politeness was a flexible concept. As Sir Lewis Namier has eloquently explained,

> Classes are the more sharply marked in England because there is no single test for them, except the final incontestable result, and there is more snobbery than in any other country, because the gate can be entered by anyone, and yet remains for those bent on entering it a mysterious, awe-inspiring gate.

The new ideals were far from being open to all, and Shaftesbury is merely more revealing than most when he recommends the "free play of mind" among gentlemen but remarks that the "mere vulgar of mankind" often stood in need of "such a rectifying object as the gallows before their eyes."[19]

The great achievements of eighteenth-century polite culture were plain to see then and many of them are still impressive. Yet the tone of the above quotation from so brilliant, enlightened, and liberal an aristocrat as Shaftesbury is telling. The fear of the mob and of a revival of the previous century's conflicts can never be overestimated. Attention to politeness had a powerfully defensive as well as a positive side. There was an awareness of its precariousness and fragility. Even in polite circles themselves you could not be too careful, particularly in the increasing number of situations where the fixity of court or rural roles could no longer be relied on. Chesterfield warns his son never to allude to the family of a person to whom he is introduced because you never knew for certain now what relationships and attitudes might exist. There is often a sense that tolerance, good humor, and restraint are being emphasized because of the need to paper over the cracks.[20] No wonder that Steele wrote: "in all the little Intercourses of Life . . . a Man ought to sacrifice his private Inclinations and Opinions to the Practice of the Publick" (Spectator No. 576); that Budgell advised: "Avoid Disputes as much as possible" (Spectator No. 197); or that Shaftesbury put forward good manners as the precise antidote to the divisive effects of religious zeal ("Letter Concerning Enthusiasm").

The emphasis on politeness and refinement always takes place, of course, against a backcloth of appalling social conditions. Primitive hygiene and medicine and high rates of infant mortality affected all classes. Bathing was rare and the streets full of filth. "What we have above all lost from the world we have lost," writes Roy Porter, "is the stench: eyes were less offended than noses, for much was invisible in a world lit by candles and rush-light." If London was the place of fashion it was also the place of Gin-Lane and Grub Street, of crime and terrible poverty. Eighteenth-century politeness obviously depends on exclusion, on the definition of a "low Other," a source of contamination, dirt, and danger, but also in some respects the object of horrified fascination. Strenuous attempts were made, for example, to restrain and control the excesses of popular festivities in the period, but despite the fact that polite culture tried to define itself *against* the popular, the two realms were embarrassingly close at times all the same.[21]

Theories and Strands

Politeness was also problematic at a more theroetical level. The old ideology implied a normative link between high birth and moral status, and presented manners more generally as the fixed mores of a stratified society. The new, broader-based, upper-class values seemed divorced from moral responsibility. At the same time, split off from the traditional complex, the conventional sentiment that virtue is the only true nobility now attains more genuinely critical force in a "middle-rank" moralism. Both the decline in the old aristocratic ethos and the changes brought about by consumerism contributed to the slide from manners as the mores of a traditional society to manners as politeness. The feeling grew that the new developments could not easily be comprehended within the old criteria. The realm of economics, even the social and public sphere as such, seemed to have become more autonomous and secularized. If politeness was evidently bound up with consumerism and fashion and hence with the prosperity of the whole nation, then how did this relate to traditional condemnations of luxury?[22] How could traditional aristocratic ideas about leisure be related to the growing sense of the importance of labor and business brought about by the emphasis on agrarian improvement and the financial revolution?

The deliberately amoral cynicism of Mandeville's defense of politeness and commercial prosperity is obviously the most extreme index of the potential threat to the traditional ethos. Much more typical is the way that, as Lawrence Klein has shown, Shaftesbury attempts to retain as many traditional aspects of virtue in the new society of transactions as he can.[23] Later writers in the century will be less defensive, taking up Mandeville's ideas without his cynicism as they claim that commerce itself civilizes, though they too have their ambivalences and scruples. For, as Aaron Hill writes to Thomson, "Think seriously . . . and try, if in all your intimate acquaintance with past ages you can find a people long, at once, retaining *public virtue* and *extended commerce*."[24] A classical theory of development that is very influential in the period looks to a progress toward sophistication and then to a steady decline into luxury and corruption. Those who look back to the stability or putative stability of landed order or scrutinize the new developments from the perspective of "civic humanism," i.e., the *vertu* of the independent landowner, will obviously be hostile to what they regard as the slippery politeness of a commercial society. Swift and the later Pope come logically enough in the end to condemn "politeness" itself as a false art grown luxurious, the last decadence of a civilization,[25] though this does not of course mean that they have lost their concern for manners in the deepest sense.

The ideals of classical stoicism and "simplicity" by which the oversophistications of commercial luxury are condemned are also, however, often employed to justify attention to manners and to provide a more solid rationalistic basis for them. In the popular theories of "civility," sometimes termed "good breeding," the "ceremonies" of any particular society are differentiated, as in classical stoicism, from the natural and universal rules of social behavior taught to all men by reason. "Civility," praised by Pope and Swift, can thus incorporate those who are not highborn. But if this is a demystification in one sense, it also reconfers mys-

tique in another. The ideological attempt to underpin politeness
by reason does not make it any more democratic. Natural civility
might be universal, but particular ceremonies could not simply
be ignored. It was still necessary when in Rome to do what the
Romans did. Dr. Arbuthnot amusingly personified the Church of
England in this respect as a woman who was "well bred without
Affectation, in the due mean between one of your affected Cur-
tesying pieces of formality, and your romps that have no regard to
the common Rules of Civility."[26] Social expertise could really be
learnt only in the best circles, and the "reason" required was
itself partly a function of a traditional classical education.
Chesterfield's ploughman might be theoretically capable of learning the graces, but in practice he had very little opportunity of
doing so. The apparent appeal to a lowest common denominator
is thus always complicated by a recognition of the superiority of
the polite world to the rest.

The strong cult of sincerity in the period is another attempt to
combat the artifices and insincerities of society. It is obviously a
part of that "affective individualism," the emphasis on personal
feeling and the domestic virtues, that Lawrence Stone regards as
the most important cultural development of the whole period.
Though he no doubt exaggerates the specifically bourgeois force
of these influences, bourgeois elements were certainly involved.[27] "Sincerity" can also overlap with the Protestant moralism that is a potent, if sometimes neglected, factor in the period.
"Sincerity" is cultivated in deliberate opposition to the worldling
or courtier with his artificial manners. It goes together, in its
early phases, with an attack on that Restoration libertinism by
which, according to Jeremy Collier, a "fine Gentleman" had come
to mean only a "fine, Whoring, Swearing, Smutty, Atheistical
Man."[28] In the fourth book of The Family Instructor Defoe similarly rejects the whole world of fashion. "Sincerity" is also
linked with arguments for the toleration of Dissent, as in Arthur
Maynwaring's ballad attacking the Occasional Conformity Bill,
"for if so be the heart's sincere, /Oh that is all in all."[29]

Anglicans and Dissenters worked together in the Societies for
the Reformation of Manners to police morals and stamp out
drunkenness and swearing.[30] A marked prudishness is apparent
in some quarters, though it obviously coexisted with remarkable
freedom in others. The Scots Magazine for 1739 pointed to a
significant change in the drama:

So far is the dirty ribaldry that once could alone please, from being
countenanced now, that seldom a double entendre is allowed, three

of which if apparent to the spectators would be enough to damn a play of considerable merit.[31]

It is difficult to disentangle the specifically moral and religious elements of this from the more purely social side of the "civilizing process," the according of respect by fastidiousness, the desire to "separate one's body and its juices and odours from contact with other people, to achieve privacy in many aspects of one's personal activities, and generally to avoid giving offence to the delicacy of others." Both influences obviously overlap when Richardson's Lady Jones is made to say to Sir Simon in *Pamela* that "A Gentleman of your Politeness would not say anything that would make ladies blush."[32]

Richardson is at least traditional enough in seeing that matters of politeness are very much involved with relations between the sexes. Ideological revisions obviously became necessary here too. Traditional Platonic and courtly idealism diminished with the growth of new movements in philosophy, changes in the court, and the effects of bourgeois influence. Patriarchal attitudes were softening for similar reasons. A real, if limited, liberalization of attitudes to women was part of the general complex of social and political enlightenment. Meanwhile new conditions of labor made domestic manufacture redundant and so reduced women's productive economic role.[33] At the same time the *rentier* and commercial ethos made a conspicuously well-dressed and leisured wife an index of gentility and success.

The new prosperity and leisure created a wider feminine audience for literature. A self-conscious refinement of tone is cultivated toward the "very politest and tenderest Sort of Readers."[34] This represents an alliance between a modified version of courtly language, an emphasis on the more passive domestic virtues associated with the newer "affective individualism," and elements of bourgeois sentimentalism. But as Ellen Pollak has remarked, the new myth of woman "was not self-evidently more benevolent than earlier attitudes simply because it presented itself that way." The new sentiment often disguises or is accompanied by a patronizing tone or the "polite disparagement" of women.[35] It is related to the attempt to internalize controls. James Thomson, for example, dissuades the "BRITISH FAIR" from hunting, with its "masculine Attire" in which "all / The winning Softness of their Sex is lost":

In them 'tis graceful to dissolve at Woe;
With every Motion, every Word, to wave

Quick o'er the kindling Cheek the ready Blush;
And from the smallest Violence to shrink
Unequal, then the loveliest in their Fears;
And by this silent Adulation soft,
To their Protection more engaging Man.

. . . .

Well-order'd Home Man's best Delight to make;
And by submissive Wisdom, modest Skill,
With every gentle Care-eluding Art,
To raise the Virtues, animate the Bliss,
Even charm the Pains to something more than Joy,
And sweeten all the Toils of human Life.
This be the female Dignity and Praise.[36]

Addison and Steele were regarded as particularly successful in cultivating a female audience. This was an essential part of their polite ideology, the comprehensiveness and centrality of which can hardly be exaggerated. They told Lord Somers that their periodical endeavored to "cultivate and Polish Human Life, by promoting Virtue and Knowledge, and by recommending whatsoever may be either useful or ornamental to Society."[37]

The *Tatler* and the *Spectator* played a major role in the creation of the "public sphere" of relatively free discourse, secular, non-hierarchical and unimpinged upon by the State. Yet this whole development depends on and results from the weakening of other final authorities. Because of this Addison and Steele, in a brilliant mystification, use public opinion—consensus—as their source of authority in the very act of helping to create such a consensus. The mode of free, apparently random discourse is used to disguise an ideological program, or rather is its entirely appropriate medium. "Addison and Steele," it has been said, "more successfully than any preceding English writers translated the tone of civilized oral exchange into print. The easy flow of written speech became not only their literary signature but their avowal of communal identity."[38]

This, like the social life it mimics, is a genuine, perhaps an enviable cultural achievement. But the whole process is a deeply political and ideological one. The relaxation of the stiffness of absolutist rank is a Whig emphasis, but freedom only goes so far. The whole manner of these essays enacts their values of stylishness, good humor, political and religious "moderation," and avoidance of fanaticism. The terms of entrance to the club are enacted and implied rather than spelt out, but they have to be learnt if they are not instinctively known already. They are rela-

tively broad terms, but they still exclude many. Lee Andrew
Elioseff writes that:

> Addison addressed that part of the affluent and upward-mobile mid-
> dle class usually at least nominally Church of England . . . interested
> in the cultural and fashionable tastes of their betters, ready to "im-
> prove" themselves by reading or reading about important literary and
> intellectual works. . . . His appeal was not to the small middle-class
> tradesman.[39]

The whole endeavor amounts to a "totalizing project of moral
education."[40] It pays the clearest and most self-conscious attention to what seem the relatively trivial details of dress and behavior, providing cultural guidelines of extraordinary range and
detail, which encompass *Paradise Lost* and fans, attitudes to
witches and the Royal Exchange. At the heart of the whole
program, as has often been remarked, is the attempt to ac-
climatize and remove fears about the new commerce, the effects
of overseas trade and "Public Credit," the subject of a famous
allegorical vision in *Spectator* No. 3. These essays adjudicate
with the greatest of care between the traditional landed classes
and the merchants, between traditional moral criteria and a recognition of the need for enlightened self-interest in the new
economic conditions, and between justifiable and reprehensible
forms of luxury and extravagance.

Addison and Steele thus need to invoke religious sanctions
and controls in conditions seen to be in some senses threateningly secularized without at the same time calling up a dan-
gerous enthusiasm or an old-fashioned moral condemnation.
They try to heal the damaging seventeenth-century split between
courtly social refinement and Protestant seriousness. They attack
the decadent Restoration ideal of the gentleman on the one hand
and Protestant fanaticism on the other, and look forward to a time

> when it shall be as much the Fashion among Men of Politeness to
> admire a Rapture of St. *Paul,* as any fine Expression in *Virgil* or
> *Horace:* and to see a well dressed young Man produce an evangelist
> out of his Pocket and be no more out of Countenance than if it were a
> Classick Printed by *Elzevir.*[41]

Yet they cannot fully fuse things together again. They fear the
results of secularism, yet themselves wish to preserve a certain
moral autonomy for the economic sphere. Their versions of
Christianity run the risk of falling into moralism at one extreme

and an overvaluing of social style at the other. When Steele gives his famous praise to Swift, the anonymous author of a *A Project for the Advancement of Religion and the Reformation of Manners*, as one who "writes like a Gentleman, and goes to Heav'n with a very good Mien," he can hardly avoid the suspicion that he is attaching too much weight to social factors.[42]

Addison and Steele present Christianity not as a narrow way but as a broad path of consensus and compromise for the period. It is an index of Swift's terrible disaffection as well as of the embarrassing quality of his genius that he is elsewhere able to voice the insight, shrouded in layers of irony though it be, that the restoration of "real Christianity"

> would indeed be a wild Project; it would be to dig up Foundations; to destroy at one Blow *all* the Wit, and *half* the Learning of the Kingdom; to break the entire Frame and Constitution of Things; to ruin Trade, extinguish Arts and Sciences with the Professors of them; in short, to turn our Courts, Exchanges and Shops into Desarts: And would be full as absurd as the Proposal of *Horace*, where he advises the *Romans*, all in a Body, to leave their City, and seek a new Seat in some remote Part of the World, by Way of Cure for the Corruption of their Manners.[43]

2

"This Potent School of Manners": Politics, the Poet, and Mores

Polite Poets and the Commercialization of Literature

Both its admirers and its detractors have called eighteenth-century poetry "polite." If the word is taken to be synonymous with "elegant," then the description may be patronising and misleading. But early eighteenth-century poetry has its roots in two conservative Renaissance traditions with the deepest relevance to manners—the poet as sanctioned commentator on mores and the court amateur mode. It continues these traditions in its own comments on manners and in its marked concern for social tone, but it also, of course, reflects the problematic aspects of politeness in the period.

When Dryden uses the image of polishing and repolishing a gem, he is revealing the concentration on judgement and revision that neoclassicism highlights.[1] But the word "polish" shifts constantly between artistic and social uses. The great majority of the poets of the time are assimilated to an upper-class ethos by birth, education, or the need for patronage. Hobbes pointed out that the "Readers of Poesie" are also "commonly Persons of the best Quality."[2] In phrases like "polite letters" the artistic sense of polish is very obviously a social one as well because of the elite bias of a classical or "liberal" education. Dudley Ryder writes with self-improving earnestness, "One cannot read any book I believe more fit to learn one the polite way of writing and conversing than Horace."[3]

The ideal of polite conversation is itself crucial in bringing together a broader-based elite and in protecting susceptibilities in the interchanges of London:

But Wit and Genius, Sense and Learning join'd
Will all come short if crude and unrefin'd;

'Tis Converse only melts the stubborn Ore,
And polishes the Gold, too rough before.[4]

But if Horace's conversational model is thus an especially relevant one for poets of the time, the situation is not the cosy one
portrayed in old textbooks. A complex and interlinked series of
changes in politics, in politeness, and in attitudes to the sale of
literary works were creating the need for urgent readjustments in
traditional, ultimately aristocratic, roles.

The politicization of the elite had given a great boost to print,
as the demand for political pamphlets during the civil wars
contributed to the rise of periodicals and a general increase in the
market for books. The audience for poetry itself remained a
conservative and relatively small one, and it was less affected by
the so-called commercialization of literature than the other
kinds. Yet the tantalizing prospect of making some money by
sales began to exist. Gay received £1,000 from the booksellers for
a volume of his poems, though this was largely on the strength of
The Beggar's Opera. The use of the model of polite conversation
shows poets feeling their way in establishing a relationship in
the new conditions. They wish to preserve the intimacy between
poet and reader that had been possible in the old amateur manuscript tradition, but the preservation of the old modes is necessarily now something of an attractive fiction.

It is nevertheless a remarkable index of the conflation of aristocratic and commercial values that these conventions survive into
the age of Grub Street. The court's domination of literature during
the Renaissance had given this essentially aristocratic, leisured,
amateur tradition a strong influence. Courtly sprezzatura included the idea of an apparently effortless ease in the turning of
verses and an aristocratic disdain for what has been called "the
stigma of print" associated with selling one's work in the mar-
ketplace.[5]

The amateur tradition is necessarily also an occasional one,
since amateur poets are likely to write only "occasionally" and
will not therefore make the ambitious claims that poets of full-
time dedication make. As Prior's friend Charles Montagu, later
the Earl of Halifax, writes,

I know my Compass and my muses size,
She loves to sport and play, but dares not rise.[6]

The title Poems on Several Occasions, which remains surprisingly popular in the early eighteenth-century, continues to

carry something of this self-depreciating sense, but the poetic
modesty is also, of course, a social pride. Widening, relatively
superficial criteria for politeness and membership in the elite
gave nonaristocratic poets enough social status to be touched by
the traditional prejudices. But the courtly amateur pose also
obviously helps poets to make the best of it when traditional
patronage is less available, and to conceal their own attempts to
make money by sales.

Even those who have no claim whatever to the status of quasi-
aristocratic amateur continue to adopt the conventional pose in
an attempt to disarm criticism. John Oldmixon published under
the *Poems on Several Occasions* title in 1696 (London) and
insisted on the pose in his preface, "Poetry has not been the
Business of my life; I should reckon it among my Misfortunes if it
had." In Henry Carey's preface to his *Poems on Several Occasions* (1713, 3rd edition, London) he wrote that he published
because "some of the following pieces [had] the Good Fortune to
please several of my Friends," and that poetry had been "my
Amusement, not my Profession." This from a man who hanged
himself in destitute despair after a lifetime of trying to make a
living as a writer!

The distinctively eighteenth-century turn given the tradition is
shown in the phrasing of an English translator of Gracian, "And
tho' a Gentlemen be too prudent to make Poetry his Business or
Profession, yet he has not as little of the Poet in him but he can
make a Copy of Verses upon occasion."[7] A paradoxical overlap
occurs between the old aristocratic *sprezzatura* and what might
be considered the early bourgeois distaste for wasting time on
poetry at all. The latter is described, for example, in Parnell's
"The Flies, an Eclogue" and Lady Winchelsea's "A Tale of the
Miser and the Poet":

> Quoth *Mammon*, pray Sir, do not wrong 'em;
> But in your Censures use a Conscience,
> Nor charge Great Men with thriftless Nonsense:
> Since they, as your own Poets sing,
> Now grant no *Worth in any thing*
> *But so much Money as 'twill bring.*
> Then never more from your Endeavours
> Expect preferment, or less favours.
> But if you'll scape Contempt, or worse,
> Be sure put Money in your Purse.[8]

Prior seems to assimilate the new emphasis to the older tradition, replacing aristocratic disdain with the preoccupations of an

important man of affairs and hoping that the reader of his poems will:

> make Allowance for their having been written at every distant Times, and on very different Occasions; and take them as they happen to come, Public Panegyrics, Amorous Odes, Serious Reflections, or idle Tales, the Product of his leisure Hours, who had Business enough upon his Hands, and was only a Poet by Accident.[9]

The New Politics and the "Laureate" Role

Developments toward the commercialization of literature are obviously only one part of a more general upheaval. What has recently been called the "comprehensively 'revolutionary'" period of the first half of the seventeenth century was followed by a process of consolidation that itself involved new attitudes to politics and complex ideological revisions. The political role of the poet in the new conditions became a matter of particular concern. Some of the new anxiety and ambivalence find a focus, for example, in the image of Horace himself, as recent scholarship has emphasized. If he is proposed as a model of decorum, he is also used as an example of the more pejorative aspects of corrupt politeness and of political timeserving.[10]

The most elevated and responsible conception of the poet's ideological role is the image and aspiration of the "laureate poet" on the model of Horace and Virgil, Ariosto and Ronsard, Spenser and Ben Jonson.[11] Poets who see themselves in this way do not claim to be the social equals of the court amateurs. They are prepared to publish their works like other humanist intellectual discourse, though not with the expectation of making a living by sales.[12] Instead they expect patronage from the court and aristocracy in return for their service of providing an imaginative mirror of ideal norms for their patrons.

The exemplary mode for this tradition is epic. Pope quotes Bossu in the preface to The Odyssey: "The Epic Poem is a discourse invented by art, to form the Manners, by such instructions as are disguis'd under the allegories of some One important Action."[13] Davenant is more specific about the political ideology of heroic poetry, suggesting that "Princes, and Nobles being reform'd and made Angelicall by the Heroick, will be predomanant lights, which the People cannot chuse but use for direction; as Glowormes take in, and keep the Sunns beames till they shine, and make day to themselves".[14] But this responsibility may be discharged in other poems besides epics. In Jonson's shorter poems the poet is still, as he says, a "master in manners." Following the example of Horace, seventeenth-century poets write satire, a traditional corrective of morals and manners, or "heroic occasional verse"[15] of near-epic authority, like Marvell's Horatian ode or several of Milton's sonnets.

Renaissance poets of the laureate tradition can draw on a rich ideological background for their purposes. Spenser, for example, uses classical models, Renaissance humanism, Protestant idealism, nationalism, the symbolism of court ceremony, and royal and aristocratic ideologies in his aim of fashioning a "gentleman or noble person in vertuous and gentle discipline."[16] Their work depends on the ancient framework of ideal aristocratic norms; and mores have social, political, and religious dimensions even in the somewhat bleaker version of Jonson. When he calls Lady Aubigny "Of so great title, birth, but vertue most, / Without which all the rest were sounds or lost,"[17] he is giving the premium to virtue, but he is certainly not discounting the other factors. To make mores simply equal morals would be to destroy the connection between gentle birth and gentle behavior and to minimize the importance of the social dimension. To make mores simply equal manners in the modern sense would on the other hand be to trivialize the social system by removing its ordained ethical supports. The full ideology demands, in other words, that our "betters" be our betters both morally and socially, for it is really only that double justification which can protect their position.

It would be wrong to make the position of these "laureate" poets seem a comfortable one. Spenser himself grew deeply disillusioned in the last part of his career, and Jonson's position was rarely secure. He furthermore had to face the problem of a catastrophic decline in the prestige of the court. But despite this he can still feel confident enough to address the court as "the special fountain of manners," while, as the sophisticated system itself permits, distinguishing

> . . . The better race in court,
> That have the true nobilitie call'd vertue,

from those

> Who with their ofish customes and forc'd garbes
> Would bring the name of courtier in contempt
> Did it not live unblemish't in some few.[18]

This system had united poetry with the social and political order and given a rich ideological grounding to both. Its gradual breakup required considerable readjustment, particularly for the greatest, most ambitious, and idealistic poets, and in a sense poets have never regained so important and central an ideological role.

Already in the early work of Edmund Waller a weakening of the traditional ideological sanctions is reflected in a more narrowly defined public verse appropriately considered "polite." Philosophical changes were making the old system of hierarchical correspondences redundant and the development of an opposition movement with real authority had damaged the court's confidence and its sense of absolute cultural centrality.[19] Waller's court and political panegyrics contain elaborate hyperboles and mythological allusions, but there is an air of detachment that makes it impossible to take it all very seriously.

In "Of His Majesty receiving the news of the Duke of Buckingham's death," for example, Charles I is compared both to the classical gods and to God the Father:

Where thy immortal love to thy blest friends,
Like that of Heaven, upon their seed descends.
Such huge extremes inhabit thy great mind,
Godlike, unmoved, and yet, like woman, kind!
Which of the ancient poets had not brought
Our Charles's pedigree from Heaven, and taught
How some bright dame, compressed by mighty Jove,
Produced this mixed Divinity and Love?

But as Warren Chernaik explains, "In reading we correct for hyperbole. We are not expected to believe that Charles I is in a literal sense a descendent of the olympian gods or the equivalent in action of the Christian God. Rather, the metaphorical associations serve the end of persuasion."[20] There is indeed a distinctively modern distance in Waller from the mythology of the "ancient poets," and this is brought out in the slightly arch diction of "some bright dame compressed" by Jove. Waller is paying compliments through his elaborate allusions rather than expressing by them truths felt to have an ideal and symbolic reality. The formal and elevated style achieves an air of ceremony that is as much a matter of surface as of substance, and the metaphor of polish Waller himself uses has an especial appropriateness:

Lines not composed, as heretofore in haste,
Polished like marble, shall like marble last.[21]

The rise of Puritanism was a major factor in displacing some of the moral authority of the court and enabling a significant section of the wider elite to turn Christian idealism against it. According to Marvell it was the civil wars and their aftermath that finally made a Ciceronian moral commitment to public life impossible: "These vertues now are banisht out of Towne, / Our Civill Wars have lost the Civicke crowne."[22] It is a measure of the depth of the crisis that John Milton writes what is in one sense the greatest of all the Renaissance laureate poems in "isolation from the institutions of power."[23] His example is thus both awe-inspiring and deeply problematic for conservative poets.

The apparently complete restoration of the traditional institutions in 1660 did not prevent the court of Charles II from displaying all the symptoms of the ideological crisis the old order had passed through. The court wits with their cultivation of a deliberately decadent *politesse*, "Mannerly Obscene," indicate a devastating disruption in conservative traditions of mores:

> The court of Charles II itself made a farce of the chivalric and classical icons of aristocratic and regal identity. The defiant, transgressive devilry of the Restoration court seemed to betoken a crisis of nobility after the civil wars despite the control and political influence which it had maintained.[24]

Among the wider elite of the well-educated and prosperous in the country at large, old ideologies and attitudes to politics had to some extent been displaced during the seventeenth century by what has been called a new "civic consciousness." The civil wars, the appeals made to both sides in the Exclusion Bill Crisis, and the 1688 Revolution furthered the development of new ways of looking at politics. The rise of party politics was a natural completion of the process by which politics was becoming a more secularized and autonomous realm. To a very remarkable degree, however, as J. C. D. Clark has shown, the old order was able to assimilate these developments, after the initial traumas, without endangering its own position. Aristocratic power was reasserted at the same time as it was reinterpreted, and this blends in with, softens, and controls the effects of the growing importance of criteria akin to our modern sense of public opinion.[25]

Nevertheless these developments, while increasing the demand for political poetry, made the *gravitas* and the apparently objective stance of the traditional mode harder to sustain. For Dryden this problem of the political role of the poet is obviously the central one. He is very much a court poet and a conscious spokesman for court values. He asserts the authority of a conservative hierarchy, yet he can hardly appeal to the old, transcendent sanctions in Charles II's court without a certain irony. His praise of a court audience for fine conversation and gallantry is more purely social than Ben Jonson's and reflects the ethos of post-Restoration politeness. He announces of the court that " 'Tis necessary for the polishing of Manners to have breath'd that Air," though he adds wryly, "but 'tis infectious even to the best Morals to live always in it."[26] He finds himself above all in a situation in which the court has itself become much more clearly than before a political party, with an opposition party to counter.

Following Waller, Dryden uses traditional imagery that implies all the old sanctions with a recognition at the same time that such imagery is no longer literally credible:

> The hope was that this anachronistic usage might revalidate the former correspondential parallels between the King and God or Christ, thus implying tendentiously a divine authority for a particular polity or ideology.[27]

Despite the difficulties of his situation, Dryden's best work in the public mode triumphantly combines wit and topicality with full seriousness. He is able to preserve and pass on to Pope the centrality of the dedicated poet's public role, for " 'Tis no shame to be a Poet, tho' 'tis to be a bad one."[28] His later enforced departure from the court and from active political involvement, however, was a graphic example of the practical as well as the theoretical difficulties the new politics caused poets. From this time on, with rare exceptions, "official" court poetry becomes almost impossible to write and degenerates into the "birthday songs" mocked by Pope and Swift.

For two or three decades at the end of the seventeenth and the beginning of the eighteenth centuries, the new party politics created a specific kind of patronage, with poets serving as journalists, propagandists, or party diplomatic appointees like Prior. As one commentator wrote, "We see men of Polite Parts snatch'd up from Pen-Ink Labours to the greatest Employment in the Government, made Parliament-men, Commissioners, Secretaries of State etc."[29] But this system presented its own problems. Such patronage was not granted so that these poets might write poetry, but that they might display their talents in other ways, perhaps with a political poem thrown in from time to time. And as Prior several times pointed out, changes in administration could ruin the careers of those who had been too partisan.

If the tradition of court poetry continues only in decadent form in "birthday songs" to kings and queens, a more central and ambitious attempt to write affirmatively on politics and mores is the mode that has been called "Whig panegyrical poetry."[30] Its practitioners attempted to take over the rhetoric of Milton and apply it to the celebration of the wonders of liberty, prosperity, commerce, Newtonian science, and English Protestantism. They are self-consciously "moderns" in their praise of the realities of the new society, but also, despite their use of georgic models, in their belief, with the example of Milton behind them, that modern English Christian poets can outdo the classics in sublimity. Sir Richard Blackmore even argues that classical epics cannot possibly be relevant in improving modern manners.[31]

As with Blackmore, this mode may seem largely absurd in its self-conscious sublimity and poetic enthusiasm, its turning of Milton to secular purposes that now seem mundane, and its blatant propagandizing that makes King Arthur, for example, a model for William III, the Protestant champion.[32] But the mode was not exclusive to Whig poets. The end of "Windsor Forest," for example, it indebted to it. Moreover it includes a poet of the stature of James Thomson, whose preface to Winter invokes Moses, Milton, Blackmore, and the whole tradition of the religious sublime. Thomson's is the most successful of the secularizations of Milton since his chosen subject—nature—is appropriately the object of the religious awe of the physico-theologians, yet also the vehicle for the widest possible variety of reflections on culture and civilisation, human sexuality, agriculture, and labor ("Ye generous BRITONS, venerate the Plow!")[33]

Recent critics have shown how this central motif of nature enables various evasions in Thomson's work and conceals contradictions in attitude to the aristocracy and to primitivism and civilization. Thomson is a poet of the highest ambitions. He spells out in the clearest possible terms his sense of the poet's responsibility over mores. He calls poetry "this potent School of Manners," and elsewhere imagines:

. . . the dread delightful School
Of temper'd Passions, and of polish'd Life,
Restor'd.[34]

But at the heart of his concern about modern manners lies his worry about the growth of a commercial society. Time and time again he praises commerce and recognizes its centrality as the basis of modern English prosperity, but he also speaks of a country dominated by interest and corruption, where the arts are in danger. He obviously shares the concern he attributes to Lyttelton for "BRITANNIA'S Weal; how from the venal Gulph / To raise her Virtue, and her Arts revive" (Spring, 930–31). He wishes in other words to divorce the moral effects he discerns from their cause, which he praises. In a revealing letter to Aaron Hill he calls commerce "the kind Exchanger of the Super-abundance for the Sweets and Elegancies of Life" and says it is only the "Want of Taste" that has poisoned the well.[35] Despite his deeply felt reservations, his poems remain strongly affirmative, and no others in the mode so energetically celebrate and so successfully act out in the expansive enthusiams of blank verse the dynamics of the new order.

The work of Thomson is a major attempt to unite ethics and politics and to speak centrally and affirmatively in the new conditions. But the mode of Whig panegyrical poetry could easily degenerate into bathos. For all Thomson's intelligent reservations his mode was too warmly celebratory about modern England and in particular about commerce to be available, at least as a full-scale strategy, for more conservative poets.[36] Even those by no means opposed to the new ethos came increasingly to feel, like Thomas Blackwell and a growing chorus of opinion, that the comfort and sophistication of modern society meant that a true epic was no longer possible.[37]

Polite Sentiment

The periodical essay of Addison and Steele achieved considerable success as the organ of the new public sphere in accomodating to the new realities. Increasingly, though, as Michael McKeon has recently argued, it was the novel that was able to examine and confront all the emerging ambiguities of status and morality in the new society.[38] The old system had packaged together poetry, hierarchy, politics, religion, ethics, and social behavior. Now poetry was perhaps too narrow in its social base and too associated with classical models to adjust very easily to the new situation. Steele wrote that "Poetry is in it self an Elevation above ordinary and common Sentiments."[39] This neoclassical demand for elevated poetry can itself be inhibiting in its effects, particularly when influential commentators were saying that the age was unsuitable for epic anyway. To write on mores with a proper seriousness seemed to require either the ideological assurance of the old laureate mode or an expansive enthusiasm for the new ethos. Talented poets with aristocratic or quasi-aristocratic sympathies were attracted instead by the mode of polite occasional verse, which has already been seen to have a considerable vogue in the period. They preserve in this way a quasi-aristocratic wit and stylishness, while evading the need to write in the longer kinds.

Satire, that traditional corrective of mores, though regarded as characteristic of this period, was in fact, more troublesome than might at first appear. The growing interest in politeness both increased the demand for satire as a social guide and a check on deviants and made it more problematic, since it is, after all, a potentially impolite mode. The debate about how far the satirist should go was thus a particularly pertinent one at this time. There was the danger that satire would lose its cutting edge in the new conditions. One poet wrote complacently:

We, like Menander, more discreetly dare,
And well-bred Satire wears a milder air.[40]

The new politicization itself increased the demand for slighter, more topical occasional poems on political subjects; and these were, of course, often satirical. Yet many poets were wary of writing partisan political satire because of what could happen when governments changed. The national enthusiasm for politics on which many commentators remarked was in fact accompanied by a national disillusionment as well. An emphasis on quietist retirement from the world of who's in and who's out was inevitable among the nonjurors after 1688, but it was also apparent in other circles, if partly as an affectation. The poet Pomfret in his popular "Choice," for example, hopes never to have to meet any "busy Medlers in Intreagues of State."[41] The general interest in manners in the period, the increased social intermingling, and even this desire in some quarters for a genteel withdrawal from the world of politics thus help to produce occasional verse of a different kind, vers de société.

The verse purportedly written for a small and intimate circle can display a fashionable stylishness while evading the demands of high decorum. Freed from the more impersonal genres, "occasional" poets can turn more of their lives into poetry. An interest in something approximating to poetic autobiography appears in a poem like Prior's "Written in the Year 1696." It is in the realm of occasional verse that the new love sentiment and the cult of sincerity are most likely to be found. Even John Oldmixon writes in the preface to his *Poems on Several Occasions*, "You will find nothing in this little Volume but what was the real Sentiments of my Heart at the time I writ it."[42]

Polite sentiment ultimately seems to involve the modulation of older aristocratic influences and a blending with the new "affective individualism." A considerable degree of editing out or exclusion is apparent. These tendencies can be diagnosed with especial clarity in the work of two influential followers of the later Dryden, George Granville and William Walsh. Both are court occasional poets; both in their different ways confront the problem of new attitudes to women in the period; both seek new models of behavior and tone. Walsh recognises that the old images of court love poetry have lost their meaning, and he complains that the moderns fill their verses with thoughts that are "not tender, passionate or natural to a man in love."[43] What he has to recommend instead is a decidedly demystified, commonsense and moralistic sentiment:

> Happy the man, and only happy he,
> Who with such lucky stars begins his love,
> That his cool judgement does his choice approve.
> Ill-grounded passions quickly wear away.
> What's built upon esteem can ne'er decay.
>
> (Chalmers, 8, 407)

It is no accident that his most popular and entertaining poem, "The Despairing Lover," concerns a disappointed lover's decision *not* to commit suicide.

Granville is enough of a court poet to retain the old hyperboles, despite a lack of imaginative sympathy with their whole basis. A tone of sentimental politeness is the inevitable result:

> In vain I try, in vain to vengeance move
> My gentle Muse, so us'd to tender love;
> Such magic rules my heart, what'er I write,
> Turns all to soft complaint, and amorous flight.[44]

The old conventions undergo a peculiar transformation into mere poetic diction: the "enchantment" of a woman assumes its weakened modern sense of "charm," for example, or the imagery of imprisonment by love becomes a woman who "captivates" us. Time and again, Granville calls a woman "resistless" or talks of her "auspicious" eyes, but the words have less and less content. The residue of the old conventions creates now only an exaggerated social reverence that in Granville as in other poets of the time is often accompanied by "polite disparagement."[45]

Besides this highly artifical attitude to women, Granville demonstrates his "politeness" by suave classical allusions and a soft-flowing verse that imitates Waller. It is ultimately the function of a tremendous restriction of subject matter. The terms of his praise of Waller could hardly be more revealing:

His Eden with no serpent is defil'd,
But all is gay, delicious all and mild.[46]

To write this new kind of polite, occasional verse is to write a kind of vers de société and in so doing to provide models of social behavior. Pope felt all the personal attractions of Walsh and "Granville the polite,"[47] but their influence on him was also a literary one. He has to learn from but also to recognize the limitations of their forms of politeness, just as he adopts the attractive pose of the courtly amateur poet without reneging on his radical commitment to poetry and the public order.

3

"Alike Fantastick, If Too New, or Old": Politeness and the Dilemma of Traditionalist Poets

Traditions and Tensions

Parnell, Prior, Gay, Swift, and Pope—the group of poets at the center of this study—focus in a very special way the problems of poetry and politeness. They have a strong neoclassical sense of the demand for the poet to write serious and elevated poetry, and they also have a strong sense of their conservative ideological responsibility over mores. Yet the modification of aristocratic values, the growth of a wider polite elite, and the development of a commercial society were removing some of the ideological supports of the old system and causing a decline from traditional mores to mere politeness. Reflecting many modern influences, these poets themselves exemplify some aspects of the shift from mores to politeness, and they are cut off from the fullness of the old ideology. On the other hand, their espousal of landed interests and Renaissance court traditions puts them at odds with various aspects of the commercialization of literature, and even more with the commercial and relativist elements at the heart of modern politeness. Lacking the ideological assurance either to provide a real imaginative alternative to the new develoments or to welcome them enthusiastically, they face the danger that their poetry will be marginalized and that they will not be able to write in a serious and central way on mores at all.

Their social connections with each other are close. All but Prior belonged to the Scriblerus Club, with its self-consciously Renaissance humanist tradition of learned wit and parodies of modern learning. Prior himself, though far less intimate with Pope, was a friend of Swift's and a colleague of his in the Tory Brothers' Club. Pope showed his personal and political sympathy with Prior in his troubles after the fall of the Tories by becoming one of the prime movers in the publication of his *Poems on Several Occasions* of 1718. Recent work has also emphasized poetic links between the two men.[1]

Obviously each of these poets is strongly individual in personality and talent. It would be foolish to exaggerate their uniformity, even in their political attitudes. Yet their friendships were not an accident. They share significant poetic and cultural aspirations. This is not so much a matter of their being Tories as of their being conservative or traditionalist in a wider sense. Several of them, indeed, have Whig antecedents, and it has been said that Gay was never a Tory. But "Old Whig" or "Country" elements in their thinking assimilate well with the landed interest they espouse with varying degrees of intensity.[2] They associate themselves with the landed gentry, if not by birth, then by education, adoption, and certainly by ideology.

The traditional elite education in the classics that each of these poets has received inclines them to the ancients' party in literature and learning. They delight to attack modern presumptions. Their classicism unites with their landed bias in the cult of civic humanism, the *vertu* of the independent landowner as a safeguard against corruption.[3] Classicism and the commitment to a conservative social order also contribute to their sense of the Renaissance "laureate" tradition. They are all talented poets, and they all at least begin as ambitious ones. They each aspire at some point or in some way to the status of a laureate poet, who expects patronage from the court and the aristocracy in return for the traditional role of upper-class spokesman. Pope in a sense never gives up on this aspiration, and even Swift in his bitterness reveals the inverted influence of the tradition in his claim that now "the vilest Verse thrives best at Court."[4]

None of these poets is by background, birth, or wealth very securely a member of the traditional upper classes in the fullest sense. Parnell is from a gentry family with Cromwellian connections. The gentry families of Gay and Swift are in decline. Pope was the son of a comfortable merchant, though he believed he had aristocratic connections. Prior was the son of a London "joiner" who had prospered. In a general sense they have all profited from the spread of politeness and education to a wider elite, but their position is a complex and, indeed, in some ways a troubled one. As C. J. Rawson finely says, they reveal, like Yeats, some of the special *hauteur* of nonaristocratic poets who espouse aristocratic traditions.[5] In theory at least they are proaristocratic in their commitment to hierarchy, and they regard the aristocracy as the head of their own class. But if their gentry backgrounds or identification with the landed interest overlap with their support for aristocratic traditions, particularly in their sense of themselves as writers, they also share the middling gentry's characteristic ambivalence about the aristocracy and aristocratic ideology. They support a strong monarchy and hierarchy, but their ideal is set back in a golden age—in Swift's view, for example, in the "peaceable Part" of Charles I's reign.[6] Their reaction against the breakup of the old complex that had united high birth and moral status sometimes takes the form of a moralism that is becoming indistinguishable from a more critical "middle-rank" emphasis as such.[7] Both their own social position and the general decline of the old ideology contribute to make their sense of aristocratic traditions a somewhat truncated and demystified one.

They can never recapture the fullness of the old fusion of religion and the social order either. Prior and Gay are themselves markedly secular in outlook. Parnell tempers the religious enthusiasm of his early Protestant biblical sublime into a polite Addisonian Anglicanism. Pope and Swift make orthodox Christianity a powerful satiric weapon against the Whig Socinianism and freethinking of the new age:

SOME try to learn polite Behaviour,
By reading Books against their Saviour.[8]

But neither of them is notable for his presentation of positive religious alternatives.

For these poets reveal the marked influence of a specifically Restoration scepticism, which combines oddly at times with their gentry moralism. Despite the disapproval they sometimes express, they feel a considerable attraction to the glamor of the Restoration court wits. Prior had been a protegé of Dorset, and Pope of the Earl of Mulgrave. They even themselves at times display symptoms of the special "transgressive" Restoration inversion of true aristocratic traditions. This allies with the "declassed" or "marginalized" aspects of their own positions—as members of declining gentry families, as a Roman Catholic like Pope, or as a man of relatively mean birth like Prior. These almost secret elements must not be exaggerated, but they seem to fuel with a special energy some of their rejections of the contemporary status quo.[9]

Certainly these poets themselves participate in the general consensus of modified aristocratic values and nonaristocratic elements refined into politeness. They themselves exemplify the reinterpretation of the old ideology. Yet they also disapprove of these developments for a variety of reasons. The old-fashioned quasi-feudal version of the landed ethos they espouse is not the same as the full aristocratic ideology of the past, but it combines with their moralism and their yearning for the laureate tradition to make them condemn the irresponsibility of the modern aristocracy. Gay, Pope, and Swift come in fact to see the Whig aristocracy in alliance with Walpole and the financiers as traitors to the landed interest. Pope's appeal to "th'Integrity of Ancient Nobility" is accompanied by a condemnation of the decadent contemporary breed.[10]

The myth of the stability of landed society is their weapon against modern developments. As, in a sense, part of a broad middle rank, they have much in common with the urban "men of a middle condition," but their anxiety about their own status and their "landed" bias make it imperative to differentiate themselves from such. They disapprove ideologically, however, not of trade or merchants as such, but of the consequences of the complex system of finance, which they attribute to the "monied men." Although they sometimes praise commerce, they cannot feel that sense of optimism and enthusiasm for the new society that Thomson, among others, expresses. They come increasingly instead to deplore what they regard as the social and moral effects of a commercial ethos.[11] They cannot accept what they regard as the divorce between politics and morality or the secularisation of economics and public life. Despite their own party political involvements, they all complain about the modern party system and yearn for a transcendence of it.

In their ambivalence they are split between an old ideology and a new. Their gentry attitudes mean that they reject much of the new ethos without having a full imaginative alternative to put in its place. They are, as it were, too "polite" to be fully traditionalist and too traditionalist to be fully "polite." They seek to write on modern mores with the same range and authority as their predecessors, either ignoring or condemning as a symptom of decadence the split between manners and morals involved in politeness. But they can never recapture the ideology behind the old stratified mores, and they reflect the split in modern attitudes themselves. Unable fully to embrace either the old or the new attitudes to manners, they are thus divorced from both traditions

of serious comment on mores—the laureate role and Whig panegyrical poetry—and in danger therefore of being marginalized
as poets.

The new politics had made the true laureate role and the
patterns of court patronage that supported it redundant anyway.
These poets belong to the wrong side to obtain much court
patronage after the death of Queen Anne, although Pope received
support for the *Odyssey* translation and Gay persisted in trying
for some years yet.[12] But they were increasingly caught up in the
opposition to Walpole. The debasement of the Renaissance ideal
that still haunted Pope into a mere court office held by a man like
Colley Cibber seemed only the final insult.

Aristocratic patronage continued to some extent, but, since
these writers are deprived of their traditional court role and do
not possess independent wealth, they cannot afford not to cultivate a new audience and even to try to sell their works. They
draw from the new sense of a public sphere, but they have
conservative suspicions of it in some respects, too. Traditionally,
they are bound to disapprove of the commercialization of literature, and their own quasi-aristocratic sense of themselves is
offended by the idea of professionalism.

Polite Occasional Verse and the Limits of Politeness

All these poets conceal and evade certain aspects of their
paradoxical situation by the use of the courtly amateur pose,
besides drawing positive strengths from the tradition. Parnell,
Prior, and Gay were all published under the popular *Poems on
Several Occasions* title, and Pope published a miscellany under
the same title. Swift and Pope make cruel fun of Grub Street
writers who adopt this aristocratic pose. In the "Epistle to Dr
Arbuthnot" (44) Pope has the marvelously compact description
of the poet, "Oblig'd by hunger and Request of friends." Yet Swift
has his own peculiar version of the amateur poet's nonchalance,
and Pope himself, despite his own very great dedication to his
art, was very influenced by this tradition. In the preface to the
1717 volume he presents, half seriously and half ironically, the
whole pose of the courtly amateur:

> I confess it was want of consideration that made me an author; I writ
> because it amused me; I corrected because it was as pleasant to me to
> correct as to write; and I publish'd because I was told I might please
> such as it was a credit to please.[13]

In an obvious way, the pose attempts to conceal the fact that several of these poets make money by selling their works. It indicates, as has been noticed, the spread of initially aristocratic ideals to a wider polite elite. Poets who adopt this stance wish to signify their own social worthiness to partake in the elite's more general version of *sprezzatura*. This social aspiration destroys the old distinction between the court amateurs and the dedicated laureate poets, who do not claim the highest social status for themselves. But the role of laureate poet in the fullest sense is no longer available anyway. The courtly amateur pose thus makes a virtue of necessity when there is no money from the old sources of patronage and perhaps very little from the booksellers and the public either. At the same time, in its quasi-aristocratic *sprezzatura*, the mode expresses traditional allegiances and a disdain for the new commercial ethos of literature. In the cases of Swift and Pope in particular, it is also a kind of self-protective device, in its false modesty and nonchalance, for these deeply proud and thus vulnerable spirits.

The strong sense of the demand to produce elevated verse in the major kinds that this group feels is linked with their ideological responsibilities. Yet the obligation to produce "great poetry" in an age increasingly thought unsuitable for epic treatment can be a very daunting one. The ideological traditions to which these poets are the heirs are somewhat diminished ones anyway, and the new version of polite occasional poetry has the advantage of not requiring of them any profound ideological assurance. It associates them instead with the Restoration court wits, who had linked enthusiasm and false inspiration with the hated sectaries: "Beware *what Spirit rages in your Breast, / For ten inspir'd ten thousand are possest.*"[14] Pope and Swift had their own reasons for disliking the dissenters. Their Restoration legacy made them morbidly conscious of the dangers of false inspiration (Swift's "Mechanical Operation of the Spirits") and the false sublime (Pope's *Peri Bathous*). They link a pedestrian didactic quality, too, with Protestant piety and respectability: "Some who grow dull religious strait commence / And gain in morals what they lose in sence" ("Couplets on Wit," p. 295).

In this way the occasional mode distances these poets not only from the more ideologically assured and solemn poetry of the past but also from what they increasingly regard as the false sublimities of the present. Their own sense of themselves as members of the "ancient" party is included in their self-definition as polite gentlemen. It involves a confidence in their education and their own sense of morality. They wish to distance themselves from the pedantry of the textual scholars like Bentley, who follow the letter and not the spirit of the classics. Paradoxically then, it is such antiquarianism that is "modern." These poets in contrast are anxious to assert their own proper modernity in translating the classical ethos where possible into the modern age, and in trying to channel modern developments in traditional moral directions. They are prepared to recognize where the past has become redundant. Nevertheless, they suffer in a sense from what has been called "the burden of the past" themselves. Their admiration for the great achievements of the classical poets leads them to regard emulation, at least emulation by other poets who lack a proper sense of their predecessors, as presumptuous. They may admire Milton's work, but they mock his pretentious imitators in the Protestant sublime like Sir Richard Blackmore. They agree with Giles Jacob that the "Divine Art" of poetry had:

> lately so much suffr'd in its Reputation by the Performances of some who have thought themselves inspir'd, and whose Readers have too many of them thought the same, that the best Judges come strongly prejudic'd against any thing of this kind, as generally expecting nothing but Froth and Emptiness.[15]

All this is sharpened by politics. These poets are bound to dislike the false sublimities of official court poetry when the wrong people are in power. In Swift's "Progress of Poetry" it is a Whig poet who "for Epick claims the Bays" (83). The so-called "Gloom of the Tory satirists"[16] reflects a turning away from Whig optimism and its accompanying official sublime and panegyric, especially, the enthusiasm for a commercial society.

While the amateur occasional mode in its quasi-aristocratic stylishness and privileging of leisure indicates a truncated version of the old aristocratic traditions, it is also obviously distanced from the new valuation of commerce and labor. Poetry is, to be sure, no longer seen either as a fine flowering of aristocratic, leisured self-crafting or as a reprehensible distraction from the true vocation of a ruling class, for which aristocratic leisure once provided the necessary conditions of disinterest. It sometimes instead seems now to carry a weight of almost bourgeois disapproval as a waste of time and a distraction from business. But to these poets, that "business," especially the business of the town and the cynical business of party politics is itself presented as a weary soul-destroying realm. In georgics and Whig panegyrical poetry, eighteenth-century poets may attempt to treat the subjects of labor and commerce. But the occasional mode in the hands of poets with a genuine relationship to aristocratic traditions preserves a degree of the old aristocratic disdain for the realities of labor. Such poetry remains by and large a leisured enterprise, expressing at first an implicit and then later an explicit refusal to endorse the new emphases.

Insofar, though, as such occasional poetry is distanced from contemporary politics, commerce, and labor, it is also marginalized. It is not accidental that this is the age of the novel and the periodical essay and that several of these poets imply that poetry is itself somehow less serious than prose. Their dislike of Protestant moralism, their wit and stylishness, their need to differentiate their work from "official" solemnity—all seem to be in some degree of conflict with their neoclassical ambitions and their ideological purpose of writing on mores with full seriousness. When these poets do attempt the longer kinds, a gap may sometimes seem to exist, as in Prior's *Solomon*, between the "natural feelings of the man" and the "more elevated emotions of the poet."[17] Their frequent juxtaposition of ancient and modern is, as everyone knows, more likely to produce mock-heroic than real epic. Where they can truly produce a modus vivendi between old and new, as in *Trivia* or *The Rape of the Lock*, there is still a sense of diminishment, although in both poems an enjoyment of the pleasures and a recognition of the legitimate demands of the modern polite world come across as well. But these modern arts of living are very precarious and ambivalent achievements. The experience of Walpole's England was to make Pope and Gay change their minds anyway. If they recognize in these earlier poems that their inability to dignify modern society in epic terms does not all work to the disadvantage of the modern, they yet continue to be subject to the dangers of writing a poetry cut off from some of the new realities.

Occasional verse evades the inhibiting demands of high seriousness and does not necessitate either the ideological assurance of the past or an expansive optimism about the modern world. It preserves the domain of wit and sentiment against the forced elevations of "official" poetry. It assists these poets to deal with and yet to evade some of the paradoxes of their situation and to define their own versions of politeness in the new conditions, but it also accepts and embodies a certain degree of marginalization of poetry.

Parnell, for example, presents poetry as a classical and cultivated leisure preserve. This puts him at odds with the commercial and urban ethos of Addison and Steele, but he writes most of
his significant poetry before the break with them and does not
live to see the full implications of the new society become apparent. Prior begins with the ambition to be a political laureate, but
he is sceptical, secular, and increasingly disillusioned with politics. His occasional verse comes to reflect a withdrawal into a
private world and a personal, if exemplary, definition of stylishness and pose. Gay is a more obviously Tory poet in presenting modern politeness as diminished and comic, but he is not
Tory in having no meaningful alternative to proffer. His predelic-
tion for the slighter, occasional forms thus comes to signify a
deliberate withdrawal from seriousness and authority.

Such poetry is not, of course, without ideological significance
and intent, even if it evades the highest responsibility. It accommodates itself very well to the passing on of modified aristocratic
values and their blending with suitably refined nonaristocratic
influences. The exploration and enactment of polite social sentiment and of exemplary relationships with women is of the essence of early eighteenth-century occasional verse, and all these
poets explore this dimension. In Prior's "An English Padlock," for
example, the relationship between the poet's stylish tenderness
and the desire to replace the old patriarchal controls on women
by psychologically internalized ones could hardly be more obvious. Prior mediates a certain Restoration wit and stylishness,
but combines it easily with the new "affective individualism."
He makes a point of presenting himself as a man of the world, but
not really a rake, a sceptic but not a nihilist, risqué rather than
obscene. It is only in Swift that elements of Restoration exhibitionism are self-consciously used as a weapon against what is
seen as a specifically modern form of polite sentiment toward
women, although Swift has his own characteristic ideological
purposes too.

The allegiance of these poets to what was seen as the aristocratic party of wit certainly means that they propound a less
limiting definition of politeness than most in the period, despite
the very limitations of occasional verse itself. As with the court
wits, there is sometimes an aristocratic use of the demotic and a
deliberate explicitness set against Puritan prudery and bourgeois
sensibilities.[18] This combines with the influence of Renaissance
traditions of learned wit, especially Rabelais. To display the

stylishness and unconcern of *sprezzatura*, particularly in its debased Restoration form, may cut across the more genteel Addisonian politeness.

On the whole, though, in the earlier stages, tension is minimized. The excesses of Restoration wit are removed, and the young Pope was given the job of smoothing out and polishing both the versification and the tone of the elderly William Wycherley's poems. Wit has to be purified, as in the *Essay on Criticism*, from too much frivolity and immorality.[19] As Prior's work also shows, wit can be used to expand the boundaries of early eighteenth-century politeness rather than to attack it. Such wit is itself presented as exemplary and upper-class, but not threateningly so. It is in itself an education in tone and style for those not quite so blessed. It can be imitated, however, only by those who are already close to it. Prior does not have the conduct-book mentality and the full sense of the public sphere found in Addison and Steele.

As the political and cultural disaffection of Pope and Swift grows, however, the different elements in the proposed compound come to react against each other. As a clearer exponent of the landed interest than the others, Swift is farsighted in his early rejection of the contamination of modern mores. He comes to use an inverted form of the occasional amateur's *sprezzatura* to differentiate his work from the polite flatteries and enforced elevation of the decadent official poetry of a corrupt regime. This is not a withdrawal into a world of polite social verse, but an angry refusal to accept the abuse of poetry and its abrogation of responsibility for public order.

Necessarily Swift is involved, like the later Pope, in a obsessive definition of all the ways in which modern society is not polite. This creates real problems about how far the satirist can go in an age in which satire was often itself restrictively polite. The aim of both writers is to show the failure of eighteenth-century politeness to cover up or overcome its opposite. It is not the attempt itself that they disagree with, and their disgust at all that politeness needs to define itself against is all the keener for a deeper recognition of the difficulty of the task. Yet they seem fascinated as well as horrified, and at times display a subversive delight themselves in breaking the bounds of decorum, which the attempted distinction between true and false decorum only serves to conceal. They try as strenuously as any in the period to distance themselves from the vulgar, but they also at times, like Gay, bring against modern politeness a genuinely popular and

anarchic energy.[20] They hint thus, most appealingly in *The Beggar's Opera*, at an alliance between an older aristocratic or feudal
class and the lower orders against what is presented as a corrupt
modern aristocracy that has sold out to financiers and social
upstarts. Yet this is more of a rhetorical device than an actual
political program. They have no real alternative to suggest. Increasingly, they come to invert the very terms of the definition.
They portray as the heart of the "low Other" not the bourgeoisie
and the lower ranks, but the aristocracy and upper classes, the
"corrupt & corruptible world within the vortex of the Town &
Court," as Pope puts it—that is, the falsely and the corruptly
polite as well as the impolite.[21]

Much more successfully than Swift, though by a process of
mystification, Pope continues to be able to suggest that he condemns modern politeness as a deviation from a firmly held norm.
Pope is the only poet of the time ambitious enough to make as
central, if less systematic, a claim to be a guide to the good life as
Spenser. Beginning as a polite poet in some of the limiting as
well as the positive senses of the period, he early adopts the
occasional poet's mode as an index of general polite stylishness.
But it would obviously have been too limiting for a poet of his
genius, dedication, and ambition to have stayed within the con-
fines of an occasional amateur pose. As he himself said, " 'Tis not
the task of an Heroic Poet like myself to sing at marriages, burials,
and Christenings etc."[22] Throughout his whole career he preserves the idea of the laureate poet, with the deepest ideological
responsibility for mores. He comes to correct manners by satire,
by panegyric, and by the humanist poet's traditional embodiment of virtue in his own lifestyle. At the same time, he lays
claim to the social and literary prestige of the court amateur
tradition for himself on various occasions. As is well known, his
use of the subscription method enabled him to get the best of
both worlds, uniting the dedicated humanist tradition to an
aristocratic disdain for Grub Street and yet at the same time
making a living by his art. His Restoration inheritance and his
politics make him dislike the false sublime of contemporary
"official" verse as fiercely as Swift does. He comes to use the wit
and *sprezzatura* of the courtly amateur tradition to differentiate
his own dedicated poetry from the false decorum of its official
counterfeit.

This is a helpful strategy as his political disaffection grows, but
it cannot prevent his situation from becoming more and more
paradoxical. Ultimately, however, the fact that he continues to

write public political poetry at all shows his ideological determination to continue to have responsibility over mores in the
deepest sense. He continues to believe, in other words, although
with increasingly desperation, that to separate poetry, manners,
politics, and ethics from each other is to trivialize all of them.

4

"Softest Manners, Gentlest Arts": The Polite Verse of Thomas Parnell

From Prophet to Polite Poet

Though some have praised him extravagantly in the past, Thomas Parnell is mainly remembered now for his important friendships in the Scriblerus Club and for the influence of his "Night-Piece on Death" rather than for his actual literary achievements. But Parnell is a remarkable paradigm of the development into a polite poet. Pope's edition of Parnell's *Poems on Several Occasions*, published in 1722, three years after his friend's death, presented him as the epitome of the polite occasional poet. The volume was prefixed by a beautiful dedicatory poem to Harley, Lord Oxford, in which Parnell is described as one with "Softest Manners, gentlest Arts adorn'd." This sense of an overlap between social and literary polish is echoed in eloquent praise of Parnell by David Hume, Goldsmith, and Donald Davie among others.[1] But Parnell was not always a polite poet, and his metamorphosis into one shows in the clearest possible way the ideological as well as literary choices that had to be made.

For in 1758 Parnell's many polite admirers had a shock with the appearance of *The Posthumous Poems of Dr. Thomas Parnell containing Poems Moral and Divine*. The volume consisted of a mass of undistinguished work, largely biblical paraphrases and religious lyrics. After initial controversies about their provenance, these are now accepted as genuine "apprentice" poems by Parnell that Pope deliberately chose to discard from his edition: "What he gave me to publish was but a small part of what he left behind him; but it was the best, and I will not make it worse by enlarging it."[2] They are in modes and traditions largely alien to the work of a polite poet.

Parnell's own family background was low-church Anglican, and his father had been a supporter of the Parliamentarians.

These poems reveal the influence of earnest Protestant traditions in their heavy didactic emphasis. Parnell attempts the biblical sublime—the tradition especially embodied in Joshua Sylvester's translations of Du Bartas. In "Piety, Or, The Vision" an angel appears to the poet and gives him the unfortunate advice, "Be thy muse thy zeal." But the high flights of the true biblical sublime are always beyond Parnell. His raptures cannot be sustained, as he himself touchingly but ludicrously recognizes:

> But wheres my rapture where my wondrous heat
> What interruption makes my bliss retreat
> This worlds got in the thoughts of T'other crosst
> And the fair pictures in my fancy Lost.[3]

Almost equally unfortunate as well as equally remote from polite traditions are the attempts at a direct and artless expression of religious emotion. Of such poems *The Critical Review* said that they "seem rather to resemble the wild and nonsensical hymns of a mad moravian, than the remains of so excellent a writer as the late Dr. Parnell,"[4] and the comment combines literary, social, and religious disparagement.

But the later Parnell might well have agreed himself. He has moved toward politeness. His university training and his prominent Church of Ireland friends, including Swift, set him in that direction. The influence of Addison and Steele, for whom he contributed *Spectator* papers, taught him how to combine his Protestant moralism and personal religious earnestness with stylishness and moderation, and the Scriblerus group gave a further gloss of wit. Parnell's politeness involves the refining of non-aristocratic elements and their blending in with what remains of the aristocratic traditions. Gentry moralism and enthusiastic Protestantism, in potential conflict with upper class norms, are softened into polite compromise.

The mode of the *Poems on Several Occasions* as edited by Pope is in itself the enactment of a radical change in the image of the poet from biblical prophet to polite and stylish amateur. Readers are given a model of gentlemanliness that is sociable, classical, leisured. Many of the poems are presented, for example, as having a particular recipient in mind. This is often the effect in volumes called *Poems on Several Occasions*, where the aristocratic coterie tradition has become a fiction that flatters the gentlemanly reader by drawing him into the poet's select circle of friends. Exemplary models of social relationships are thus presented.

In "Health, an Eclogue" Damon is brought before us a "Youth from City Cares withdrawn." The nature of these cares is never explained, but they presumably relate to his profession. If the town is by implication the place of work, it is also the haunt of those luxurious and idle members of the upper classes who stay there all the year instead of engaging in their proper pursuits on their country estates:

> Let *Sloth* lye softning 'till high Noon in Down,
> Or lolling fan her in the sult'ry Town,
> Unnerv'd with Rest; and turn her own Disease,
> Or foster others in luxurious Ease.

> (39–42, p. 157)

Damon on the other hand, after his urban "Cares," retires to a "summer Seat" to welcome Health. So despite Parnell's disapproval of the modern town-dwelling aristocracy, he is unable to envisage a rural seat as anything but a retreat from the town. Like Gay in *Rural Sports*, he is torn between the feeling that the country is the basis of true values and the sense that the town is the real center of life.

This also relates to problems about leisure and labor. Parnell has a strong moralistic sense that idleness is bad. This need not be incompatible as such with an aristocratic sense of leisure. But Parnell's feeling that city "Cares" are almost unmentionable in a polite poem and his diminished sense of the importance of a rural estate mean that the only alternatives he has to offer to the idleness of which he disapproves are recreation and exercise such as hunting, fishing and gardening.

Parnell's sense of the importance of leisure is obviously itself a diminished one. It remains socially important as an index of politeness, stylishness, and status, but it has lost the richness of its ancient roots as well as its true aristocratic social basis. It is not presented, for example, as a necessary condition for the properly disinterested engagement in politics. Parnell himself was heavily involved, like Swift, in support for the administration of Harley and Bolingbroke, and he wrote several poems on political events. But Pope leaves them out of his edition, and Parnell himself requests in the "The Book-Worm" that poets "less engaged / In papers fill'd with Party-Rage" (57–58, p. 163). The realm of these poems is definitely a social rather than a political one. Leisure has become a matter of withdrawal from what is seen as the real world of action and business. Lord Bolingbroke in the *Essay on the Different Stiles of Poetry* is praised as being

"Intent to Business, and polite for Ease" (1438, p. 60). Leisure also continues to be the foundation of philosophy and virtue, but in the sense of retirement from normal pursuits, of recreation, rather than as the whole basis of a life. It is only Cicero's retreat that can provide a model, not his public life:

> Now Friends conversing my soft Hours refine,
> And *Tully's Tusculum* revives in mine:
> Now to grave Books I bid the Mind retreat,
> And such as make me rather Good than Great
>
> (65–68, "Health," p. 157)

The ethos of these poems, in other words, is no longer *fully* aristocratic. Parnell himself reflects the change from mores to politeness. The feeling is irresistible that older social values are being retained and yet unintentionally marginalized.

The case is exactly the same with poetry itself. Indeed, poetry and politeness define each other for Parnell. Both are classical, sociable, leisured. The *Essay on the Different Stiles of Poetry* describes something of a laureate function in the way the poet will stir up heroic deeds. But Parnell's description of the place of origin of such inspiration is very revealing:

> 'Tis here, that guided by the *Muses* Fire,
> And fill'd with sacred Thought, her *Friends* retire,
> Unbent to Care, and Unconcern'd with Noise,
> To taste Repose and elevated Joys,
> Which in a deep untroubled Leisure meet,
> Serenely ravishing politely sweet.
>
> (397–402, p. 59)

It is the sense of a "deep untroubled Leisure" that really defines and unites poetry and politeness. In "To Dr. Swift, on His Birth-Day, November 30th, MDCCXIII" poetry is personified as the sister of eloquence, "Her fairer sister," but "born in deeper ease, / Not made so much for bus'ness, more to please" (43–44, p. 321).

In one of Parnell's most attractive poems, "The Flies," eloquently praised by Donald Davie, the poet displays a crucial division in his mind about poetry. The flies are an image of poets, "incorrigibly vain" in singing their love songs, and associated by the imagery with the beaux in a theater audience. They are amazed to see beneath them one day teams of ants who strain and labor, " . . . with incessant Pains, / Press'd by the cumbrous

weight of single Grains." The leader of these "busy *Burgers*," the
ants, harangues the flies and tells them they should save up now
in preparation for the time when supplies run out:

> Let Bards to Business bend their vig'rous Wing,
> And sing but seldom, if they love to sing:
> Else, when the Flourets of the Season fail,
> And this your Ferny Shade forsakes the Vale,
> Tho' one would save ye, not one Grain of Wheat
> Shou'd pay such Songsters idling at my Gate.
>
> (69–74, p. 159–60)

But the flies of course ignore him.

Parnell's sympathies seem to a surprising degree with the bourgeois ants, but there is obviously a considerable identification
with the flies too. In "The Book-Worm" Parnell drinks a health to
poets and prays that "all their Days / May they have Bread, as
well as Praise" (55–56, p. 163). There is an unresolved problem
about poets and money and about poetry and commonsense. Are
poets idle and hence trivial or are they quite properly leisured?
What support do they have a right to in the new economic
conditions? Parnell's answers seem equivocal ones.

In a sense his own personal solution was the one the ant mayor
recommends, to "sing but seldom, if they love to sing," although
in the poem it cannot be taken completely at face value. But the
adoption of the mode of the polite occasional poet involves a
certain evasion of seriousness and responsibility *as a poet*. The
poems Pope selects are short, relatively light ones, far removed
from the lengthy poems of Protestant enthusiasm or the direct
emotion of the shorter religious lyrics. They do not demand the
ideological assurance required to write on mores in the full
laureate mode either. They are the vehicles only of diminished
aristocratic traditions.

Yet the way these poems privilege leisure and evade issues
about labor obviously distances them to a large degree from the
ants' values too. They are poems set in a small and intimate social
world rather than in the full public sphere of Addison and Steele.
The Battle of the Frogs and Mice has been shown to contribute a
blow on Pope's behalf in the Homer controversy with Addison
and Tickell.[5] But he writes the main body of his poems before the
break with the *Spectator* writers. He is deeply influenced by
them in many ways, but the quasi-aristocratic mode of his occasional verse represents not an attack on, but a failure to engage

with or endorse, their urban and commercial ethos. Obviously
enough he is distanced from the ambitious and lengthy celebra-
tions of Whig panegyrical poetry, too.

Parnell cannot really support either the old or the new ethos in
its fullness. He cannot recapture the tradition of mores, and
indeed himself epitomizes the change of values. But he cannot
fully accept the new politeness either, and to this extent his
poetry is marginalized. His pervasive classicism does not involve
a mock-heroic sense of modern diminishment, for the skillful
mock-heroic *Battle of the Frogs and Mice* is not in actual content
concerned with the contemporary world at all, despite its
oblique relationship to a literary quarrel. On the other hand
Parnell certainly does not attempt a quasi-epic affirmation of
modern society either. His classicism comes across instead as no
more than an index of education and good taste, and also therefore as a kind of evasion.

Polite Sentiment and Ideology

Such self-consciously stylish poems, evasive or not, are far
from being without their own ideological purposes. Parnell presents images of politeness and exemplary models of social inter-
action even in seemingly almost private poems. It was, as Reuben
Brower pointed out, the softer strands of sentiment and nature
poetry in Parnell that so appealed to readers and poets later in
the century. Several of his poems became so influential that some
critics have called Parnell a "preromantic," despite the apparent
absurdity of making that claim for a poet who died in 1718. Yet,
as I have tried to show elsewhere, there is nothing in Parnell that
goes beyond the norms of early eighteenth-century poetry.[6] His
sentiment is of a specifically polite kind. It represents, like his
politeness as a whole, an alliance between a partly unintentional
diminishment of earlier aristocratic traditions and a deliberate
refining or narrowing of nonpolite elements. It has in itself, in
other words, a clear link with his ideological intentions.

Parnell's nature poetry can certainly be assured and beautiful:

How deep yon Azure dies the Sky!
Where Orbs of Gold unnumber'd lye,
While thro' their Ranks in silver pride
The nether Crescent seems to glide.
The slumb'ring Breeze forgets to breathe,
The Lake is smooth and clear beneath,

Where once again the spangled Show
Descends to meet our Eyes below.

("Night-Piece on Death," (9–16, p. 169)

But its attractions lie not in some original or innovative quality
but in its very deliberate polish. The scene has been created like a
painting. No attempt is made to describe nature in detail. The
preconceptions are rather those of Hume, who wrote that
"nothing can please persons of taste but Nature drawn with all
her graces and ornaments, *la belle nature*," and Parnell is one of
the main examples Hume cites.[7] Shaftesbury and Addison are
the originators of this sense that a proper appreciation of nature
is part of the definition of polite taste, and this is the impression
Parnell tries to convey, too. The clarity and calm of this poetry
furthermore bears a link, especially in its Newtonian emphasis,
to an ideological sense of order. The link between Newtonian
science, Anglican apologetics, and a defence of the English constitution is a well-established one.[8] Despite the charm of Parnell's work, a certain drawing in of boundaries is always
apparent.

The "Hymn on Contentment," for example, is known to have
been one of the earliest poems in Parnell's chronological development to be found worthy of inclusion in Pope's edition. Like
Lady Winchelsea's work, it retains, in its graceful octosyllabic
meter, a touch of seventeenth-century religious lyricism, but the
rich hermetic sense of numinous presence in nature has been
turned into a Newtonian sense of order:

Then, while the Gardens take my Sight,
With all the Colours of Delight,
While Silver Waters glide along,
To please my Ear, and court my Song;
I'll lift my Voice, and tune my String,
And Thee, great SOURCE of NATURE, sing.[9]

(57–62, p. 112)

This is the only poem in the collection to preserve the idea of the
poet as religious prophet, but significantly the singer exercises
his gift only in his "Hours of sweet Retreat" (50).

In the "Vigil of Venus" translation, Parnell associates the new
love sentiment with an erotic nature poetry. Both nature and
sexuality, however, have to be tamed. The blatant sexuality of the
Pervigilium Veneris ("The Moisture that the stars distil on cloud-
less nights unfolds the maiden buds from the wet sheaths at

daybreak)[10] becomes coyer in Parnell's version, and a Newtonian cosmic patterning is imposed:

> A glossy Freshness hence the *Rose* receives,
> And blushes sweet through all her silken Leaves;
> (The Drops descending through the silent Night,
> While Stars serenely roll their golden Light.)
>
> (33–36, p. 149)

The anacreontic "When Spring came on with fresh Delight" similarly turns an apparent wildness and eroticism into the unromantic message, "cease for Souls averse to sigh" (55, p. 138).

In the popular "When thy Beauty appears," Parnell shows a special interest in blending together all the strands of love sentiment in the period and making them polite. The older courtly imagery of transcendence is turned into compliment, "All bright as an Angel . . . you dazzle my Eye," and reconciled with the new taste for sincerity, tenderness, and mild eroticism:

> But when without Art,
> Your kind Thoughts you impart,
> When your Love runs in Blushes thro' ev'ry Vein;
> When it darts from your Eyes, when it pants in your Heart,
> Then I know you're a Woman again.[11]
>
> (6–10, p. 132)

But the new polite sentiment softens rather than replaces traditional satire on women. The "Elegy, To an Old Beauty," for example, confronts a situation in which the threat of inappropriate female sexuality is such that now "Truth in spight of Manners must be told." Yet the whole awareness of the demands of politeness makes the poem significantly gentler as well as more moralistic than Restoration analogues like Dorset's "Th'Antiquated Coquet."

Parnell's central poem about women is "*Hesiod:* or, The Rise of Woman." It contains all the traditional misogynist charges, but the demands of politeness and sentiment make Parnell mask and teasingly deny his own involvement in the satire. The poem both is and is not by him. He puts the whole burden on the classical poet and frees himself to be ostensibly noncommital, a friend of "the Fair," merely warning other writers what will happen if they dare to attack them:

> Ye modern Beauties! where the Poet drew
> His softest Pencil, think he dreamt of you;

And warn'd by him, ye wanton Pens, beware
How Heav'n's concern'd to vindicate the Fair.
The Case was *Hesiod's;* he the Fable writ;
Some think with Meaning, some with idle Wit:
Perhaps 'tis either, as the Ladies please;
I wave the Contest, and commence the Lays.

(7–14, p. 125)

Parnell's reverence for the fair is thus here an ironic strategy, the epitome of that specifically polite disparagement that Katharine Rogers sees as characteristic of poems to women in the period.[12]

Once again too it is the accusation of idleness that seems to have a special fascination. On the one hand idleness is presented as normative for women, stemming from their original creation, part of the very nature of things. Yet on the other hand such "idleness" is railed against more than in Parnell's source and resented on behalf of hard-working husbands:

Men, born to Labour, all with Pains provide;
Women have Time, to sacrifice to Pride:
They want the Care of Man, their Want they know,
And dress to please with heart-alluring Show,
The Show prevailing, for the Sway contend,
And make a Servant where they meet a Friend.

Thus in a thousand wax-erected Forts
A loytering Race the Painful Bee supports;
From Sun to Sun, from Bank to Bank he flies
With Honey loads his Bag, with Wax his Thighs,
Fly where he will, at home the Race remain,
Prune the silk Dress, and murm'ring eat the Gain.

(125–36, p. 128)

Women are obviously made the focus here for a variant form of the same split in social attitudes seen earlier in Parnell. Both aristocratic and genteel *rentier* attitudes regard leisured wives as an index of gentility. Parnell both accepts this and yet disapproves of it in a more middling-gentry, moralistic way. His disapproval can really take no social form other than misogyny, however, since no alternative to female idleness seems to present itself to him.

"A Fairy Tale in the *Ancient* English *Style*" also shows polite sentiment masking a potentially divisive social critique. The strange narrative involves the healing of the deformed Edwin by the fairies and the promulgation of the moral that:

. . . Virtue can it self advance
'To what the Fav'rite Fools of Chance
'By Fortune seem'd design'd.

(187–89, p. 144)

Because of the splitting up of the old ideology, this conventional idea, which it had been able to incorporate, was increasingly, as Michael McKeon points out, the vehicle of "progressive" thought and "middle rank" complaints about a closed social system.[13] That Parnell voices it may thus express to some degree at least his own middling-gentry resentments. But, as with the misogyny of "Hesiod," he distances himself from it at the same time and disclaims all responsibility. The tale is told to him as an infant by his old nurse. Its sentiment is therefore polite not only in its distancing from the social critique but also in the way that the fairy trappings and superstitions can be enjoyed without commitment. The hint for this is borrowed from Addison:

> Besides this [the poet] ought to be very well versed in Legends and Fables, antiquated Romances, and the Traditions of Nurses and old Women, that he may fall in with our natural Prejudices, and humour those Notions which we have imbibed in our Infancy.[14]

It is in Parnell's Christian poems that the softening effect of polite sentiment is most apparent. He had his roots in a form of Protestantism that had caused the most immense disturbance imaginable to English social order, and his father had been a friend of one of the regicides. His so-called "versification" or modernization of Donne's third satire is a striking example of what it means to become a polite poet in this regard. It becomes clear that even the very verbal and metric choices felt to constitute the process of polishing Donne cannot fail to be ideological choices too. A full study would require a whole essay, but the reader notes from the very first line the watering down of a passion that in Donne is physically and thereby *religiously* intense, "Kinde pitty chokes my spleene," into Parnell's "Compassion checks my spleen." "I must not laugh, nor weepe sinnes, and be wise" is similarly given a sense of polite restraint its original does not carry in Parnell's:

> To *laugh* or *weep* at sins, might idly show,
> Unheedful passion, or unfruitful woe.

(3–4, p. 313)

Parnell replaces Donne's low and ill-tempered word "railing" in the next line with "*Satyr*," and the passionate search for "our Mistresse faire Religion" in line 5 with the decorous personification of "*Religion* (Heav'n-descended dame)." Perhaps the most revealing change is in a passage where Donne moves toward a powerful rhetorical climax:

> . . . And shall thy fathers spirit
> Meete blinde Philosophers in heaven, whose merit
> Of strict life may be'imputed faith, and heare
> Thee, whom hee taught so easie wayes and neare
> To follow, damn'd?[15]

Parnell, balancing the whole construction, tamely offers:

> And shall thy Father's spirit meet the sight
> Of Heathen Sages cloath'd in heavenly light,
> Whose Merit of strict life, severely suited
> To Reason's dictates, may be *faith* imputed?
> Whilst thou, to whom he taught the nearer road,
> Art ever banish'd from the bless'd abode.

> (17–22, p. 313)

The splendid euphemism of the last line can hardly fail to make us think of Pope's preacher who "never mentions Hell to ears polite" ("Epistle to Burlington," 150).

Of all Parnell's poems it is the "Night-Piece on Death" and "The Hermit" that have received most praise as original and preromantic pieces, and they certainly exercised great influence in the later eighteenth century. But the sentiment of these poems, so attractive to his later imitators, remains firmly attached to Christian doctrine. His hermit is a Christian contemplative and not a romantically medievalized solitary. The piety of these poems is orthodox and far from tepid, though, like Addison's, it has a public, rhetorical, and demonstrative quality. For this is a specifically polite form of Christian sentiment, a softening, refining, and chastening of his early prophetic enthusiasms. In both poems, for example, as in the "Hymn on Contentment," the allegorical or angelic personages appear only after tone and atmosphere have properly prepared for them, whereas in "Piety: Or, The Vision" from the 1758 volume the angel appears right at the beginning, so that a tone of hothouse religiosity prevails throughout. It is this sense of restraint that makes these poems acceptable to Pope, unlike Parnell's other religious verse, and he carefully arranges his selection to move from *vers de société*, love lyrics, and anacreontics to these poems of religious seriousness at the close.

The storyline of "The Hermit," based on primitive sources, is in itself a crude one. A hermit journeys forth to resolve his doubts about God's providence. On his way he meets a young man, and they are entertained by three hosts in turn. In each case the young man seems to act with striking and sometimes criminal injustice, but at the end he is revealed to be an angel and his behavior is explained and vindicated. Parnell's version refines the content of the story as well as the tone and style. In Henry More's *Divine Dialogues*, for example, the angel gives the miserly host a cup "as a plague and a scourge to the harsh inhospitable man . . . that he might fall into intemperance."[16] Parnell's version is full of that "sentiment" so prized in his period:

With him I left the Cup, to teach his Mind
That Heav'n can bless, if Mortals will be kind.
Conscious of wanting Worth, he views the Bowl,
And feels Compassion touch his grateful Soul.

(216–19, p. 176)

The polish and formality of the couplets themselves, of course, contribute greatly to the refining of the sources, and the nature description and the vocabulary of landscape gardening serve to put the whole story into an eighteenth-century context:

At length 'tis Morn, and at the Dawn of Day,
Along the wide Canals the *Zephyrs* play;
Fresh o'er the gay Parterres the Breezes creep.

(59–61, p. 172)

But the description of nature is not purely decorative. Its formality combines with the formality of the couplet and the marked symmetry with which Parnell arranges the narrative not only to create a pleasing aesthetic object but also to act out the meaning of the poem—the affirmation of order.

Yet the very charm, polish, and sophistication of "The Hermit" paradoxically make its attempt at a theodicy seem complacent and superficial in comparison with the primitive sources. The occasional poet's polite brevity claims a smooth assurance about dealing with such weighty matters in such a small compass that the rough-and-ready old fable does not itself imply. Much more

insistently than in the sources, Parnell's defense of God's providence is also a defense of the social status quo. There is something of the middling gentry's disapproval of the great magnates
in the idea that the nobleman's generous hospitality "from a
Thirst of Praise, / Prov'd a vain Flourish of expensive Ease" (51–
52). Once again we see Parnell's distance from the fullness of the
old traditions. But the social criticism has to be kept under
control. The miser is also attacked, but the very meaning of the
fable and the softening effect of the sentiment argue against and
cushion the effects of the questions the poem cannot help raising
about the distribution of wealth, "And why shou'd such, (within
himself he cry'd,) / Lock the lost Wealth a thousand want be-
side?" (109–10). It is clearly implied that for the hermit to ask
such a question is in itself to doubt God's providence. So the
angel's actions really serve to vindicate the socio-economic order
rather than to correct it. The real thrust of the poem is thus that
God is in charge of everything, and so we should not complain,
rather than the deeper biblical insight that there is injustice in
the present order, but that God will come to put it right at the
end.

"A Night-Piece on Death" was the most influential of all Parnell's poems in its effect on the "graveyard" and Gothic schools.
Ironically, though, such emotion is evoked in the poem only so
that it may be corrected. In a remarkable stroke of wit, Death
himself is made to criticize the extravagant gloom that later
writers like Robert Blair took up:

> When Men my Scythe and Darts supply,
> How great a *King* of *Fears* am I!
> They view me like the last of Things:
> They make, and then they dread my Stings.
> Fools! if you less provok'd your Fears,
> No more my Spectre-Form appears.
>
> (61–66, p. 170)

The poem, in other words, turns ironically back on itself, to
recommend an Anglican cheerfulness like Addison's. Its whole
structure is carefully arranged to move from a room at midnight
lit only by a flickering candle to the dark of the churchyard and
then to the full dawn of the resurrection.

The primacy of Parnell's Christian consolation is not in doubt.
He cannot be accused, like his successors, of "emotionally tinged
religious attitudinising."[17] But there is a curious softening or
blunting of traditional Christian insights in the poem all the

same. It is revealing, for example, that Parnell is so eager to present the afterlife as a realm of peace that he echoes the cadences of Spenser's Despair in an unintentional transposition of context:

Death's but a Path that must be trod,
If Man would ever pass to God:
A Port of Calms, a State of Ease
From the rough Rage of swelling Seas.[18]

(67–70, p. 170)

Earlier in the poem Parnell describes the graves that he sees when he enters the churchyard: those that "nameless heave the crumbled Ground," where "*Toil* and *Poverty* repose"; the "flat smooth Stones" of the "*middle Race* of Mortals"; and the "Marble Tombs" and "vaulted Arches" of the rich,

Who while on Earth in Fame they live,
Are senseless of the Fame they give.

(45–46, p. 169)

The criticism of the extravagant waste and futility of aristocratic mortuary arrangements carries social as well as religious disapproval. But W. A. Speck uses these stanzas on the different classes of graves as the heading to a chapter on the "Structure of Society in the Eighteenth Century,"[19] and this seems entirely appropriate. Traditionally, Christian *memento mori* poems deal with the theme of Death the leveller. Something of this is certainly present in "A Night-Piece" in the reminder that the great after death are unaware of their posthumous fame on earth and in the later comment that neither soul nor body needs the "Forms of Woe." All the same, the image of the hierarchy of graves takes up a considerable space in the poem and has an ideologically reassuring semipermanent status, at least on earth. The emphasis furthermore falls not so much on the idea that the rich do not need these elaborate trappings since all shall be levelled in death as on the notion that death is nothing much to worry about anyway. Since the rich and high-born assert their status even in death because of their anxiety that death will negate that status, there is surely something illegitimate about the way Parnell calms their fears.

It is true that he points out that the hopes and joys of which he speaks belong to "pious souls." But in his own early "Piety: Or,

The Vision," he had used the fear of death and of hell in the traditional way as a means of converting sinners:

'Strip the fair flesh, and call the phantom Death;
'His bow be sabled o'er, his shafts the same,
'And fork and point them with eternal flame.

(60–62, p. 294)

In the "Night-Piece" he is anxious instead to reassure and to differentiate himself from attitudes to death associated with Protestant enthusiasm and dissent.[20] No alternative to the fate of "pious Souls" is allowed to enter his politer poem. His sentiment in these poems consists of what is left of Christian feeling when those elements deemed unacceptable are filtered out.

"A Grace, a Manner, a Decorum": Matthew Prior's Polite Mystique

Prior as Polite Occasional Poet

Matthew Prior was almost notorious in his period for his humble social origins. He was the son of a prosperous London "joiner." For a time he served behind the bar of his uncle's tavern. Discovered reading Horace there, he was taken up by the generous Earl of Dorset and became his protégé. He entered upon a brilliant diplomatic career after leaving a Cambridge fellowship and reached his highest status as Minister Plenipotentiary responsible for the Peace of Utrecht.

Prior was deeply grateful for Dorset's generosity, and praises him several times as the repository of all the aristocratic virtues. Yet there are a surprising number of times when Prior invokes the conventional sentiment that high birth is of no ultimate importance. It is tempting to see these comments on the arbitrariness of high birth as the reflection of a radical scepticism resulting from his own background:

> NOBLES, and Heralds by Your leave,
> Here lyes what Once was MATTHEW PRIOR,
> The Son of ADAM and of EVE,
> Can STUART, or NASSAW go higher.[1]

This would be to go too far. Such sentiments had assumed a more critical "progressive" orientation by now, and Prior's background may have sharpened this sense, but the whole upper-class ethos of the period put less emphasis on birth than on a more general stylishness and poise.[2] A polite poise, independent of high birth, has a special centrality in Prior's life and work. His is the diplomat's stylishness, but it is far more than that. His "politeness" reflects a process of demystification and even disillusionment, and yet provides at the same time a means of coming to terms with them. Elements of "middle-rank" scepticism blend in with the fashionable scepticism of the Restoration court wits, whose example fascinates him. But the harshness of both is softened into a polite synthesis. This is presented, however, as primarily a personal achievement, although with exemplary overtones. Prior is obviously too much of a sceptic to be able to convey the fullness of the old ideology, but the specifically Restoration emphasis, despite his refining of it, also prevents full commitment to the new.

Prior associates himself with the court wits in his self-presentation as an amateur poet of *sprezzatura*, although he also expresses envy at their private means:

> Sidley indeed and Rochester might Write,
> For their own Credit, and their Friends Delight,
> Shewing how far they cou'd the rest out-do,
> As in their Fortunes, so their Writings too.
> ("Satyr on the Poets," 145–48, 1, 32)

Yet his early career shows signs of the ambition to be a true laureate poet. Indeed, he achieved something of that status under William III with poems such as "Carmen Seculare." In "An Ode, Humbly Inscrib'd to the Queen. On the Glorious Success of Her Majesty's Arms, 1706" he adopts the mantle of Spenser, not as poet of "perfect fairyland" but as public poet.[3]

But Prior also laments the decline of traditional patronage in the modern age:

> For now no Sidney will three hundred give,
> That needy Spencer, and his Fame may live.
> None of our Nobility will send
> To the Kings-Bench, or to his Bethlem Friend.
> Chymists and Whores, by Buckingham were fed,
> Those by their honest Labours gain'd their Bread
> But he was never so expensive yet,
> To keep a Creature meerly for his Wit:
> And Cowley, from all Clifden scarce cou'd have
> One Grateful Stone, to show the World his Grave.
> ("Satyr on the Poets," 184–93, 1, 34)

His own talents as a poet helped to make his career, but they did not make his career *as a poet*. It was as a diplomat that he was employed, and this was certainly no sinecure. The very need to make a living precluded a full-time commitment to poetry. In the preface to his 1708 volume, he expresses with conventional modesty the hope that the younger Dorset will find his poems the "Diversion of some of Your youthful Hours, as they have been occasionally the Amusement of some of Mine" (1, 256). He appears soon to have ceased to regret not being a full-time poet. He writes, for example, that "Poetry which by the bent of my Mind might have become the business of my Life, was by the happyness of my Education only the Amusement of it" (1, 583). From very early on in his career he had a wry, disillusioned awareness of the conditions of the new politics and of his own dependent position:

> Having the Prospect of some little Fortune to be made, and Friendship to be cultivated with the great men, I did not launch much out into Satyr; which however agreeable for the present to the Writers or Incouragers of it does in time neither of them good, considering the uncertainty of Fortune, and the various Change of Ministry, where every Man as he resents may punish in his turn of Greatness. ("Heads for a Treatise on Learning," 1, 583).

Such realism about the new politics would itself have made the laureate role impossible for him. In his attempts at laureate poems he continues to use cosmic and divine imagery, as in "On the Coronation of the Most August Monarch King James II and Queen Mary":

> See, Glorious as the *Eastern* Sun,
> Our *Monarch* from the Waters rise,
> Whilst Zealous Crowds, like *Persians* run
> To own the Blessing by their Sacrifice.
> ("On the Coronation," 29–32, 1, 2)

Such an older symbolic way of viewing the great is, despite many reservations, still *poetically* viable for Dryden. Prior's wordly disillusionment with politics is much more thoroughgoing. "Journey to Copt-Hall" seems to reveal his truer attitude to the elaborate panegyrical imagery:

> Here wel-set Simile might shine
> Of Pilgrimage to Power divine,
> Of zealous Persians who wou'd run
> To gaze on beams of distant Sun;
> But th' are abus'd by frantic *Lee*
> And sung to Stuttring *Durfey's Ge sol re.*
> (21–26, 1, 72)

His best political poems are those that parody a laureate poet, Boileau, and express a real awareness of the difficulties of the mode in contemporary circumstances:

> And tho' the Poet made his last Efforts,
> WURTS—who could mention in Heroic—WURTS?
> ("A Letter to M. Boileau," 22–23, 1, 221)

As W. B. Piper has said, Prior's work in fact shows a progression from the fierce urgency of political strife to the ceremony of polite praise of royalty and then to "a racier, more incisive utterance in which kings and queens are merely details."[4]

As a writer of a classical and conservative bias, Prior was highly aware of the poet's obligation to produce lofty public verse or dignified epic. In *Solomon* he produces such a work, but it is significantly divorced from either of the two main ideological modes for poetry of high seriousness. It is not a court epic with national ambitions. It has nothing but disillusionment with politics to express, apart from the brief and digressive praise of Britain in Book 1—an index of Prior's embarrassed recognition that such works really should have a political dimension. On the other hand *Solomon* is hardly a full biblical epic either, nor its secularized equivalent in Whig panegyrical poetry. It is the expression not of religious or quasi-religious enthusiasm but of scepticism and at most a degree of fideism at the close. Despite occasional critical praise for the poem, most readers have had the sense that this is a work in which it was "not the poet's natural emotions as a man that were called into play so much as his elevated emotions as a poet."[5]

Prior's cast of mind is a sceptical and secular one, despite an occasional worrying of religious problems in verse. He is influenced by Restoration irreverence and has a deep temperamental suspicion of the false sublime. He remarks of poets that:

> In noble Songs, and lofty Odes,
> They tread on Stars, and talk with Gods.
> Still Dancing in an airy Round;
> Still pleas'd with their own Verses Sound.
> Brought back, how fast soe'er they go:
> Always aspiring; always low.
> ("A Simile," 1, 245)

He is always aware of a potential gap between "true" prose and enthusiastic poetry, and the ironic awareness includes his own endeavors:

> Prior may say what he will in Verse, that Hymn was all
> Enthusiasm. All Heros, Stars, and Gods. In Prose I am sure
> He is of another Opinion. ("Charles and Clenard," 1, 603)

The amateur mode encourages a certain spontaneity, "an absence of pretentiousness, solemnity, and self-regard,"[6] that fits in better with Prior's talents. He can be refreshingly adventurous, producing Chaucerian and Spenserian imitations, for example. In many poems he achieves an easy, unbuttoned, and colloquial intimacy of tone, although others show playful elaboration and polish. Like the Restoration court wits he admires, he writes best in the shorter kinds. The pessimism of *Solomon* is expressed in a no less genuine but more characteristic way in a racy tale like "The Ladle":

> Against our Peace We arm our Will:
> Amidst our Plenty, *Something* still
> For Horses, Houses, Pictures, Planting,
> To Thee, to Me, to Him is wanting.
> That cruel *Something* unpossess'd
> Corrodes, and levens all the rest;
> That *Something;* if we could obtain,
> Would soon create a future Pain:
> And to the Coffin, from the Cradle,
> 'Tis all a WISH and all a LADLE.
>
> (161–70, 1, 207)

Prior became a close friend of Swift's in the Tory Brothers Club. Through Swift he met Pope, although he and Pope never became close.[7] Like others of the group he is self-consciously a poet of wit. Indeed it is that peculiar version of the aristocratic ethos espoused by the Restoration court wits with which he most identifies. Like Parnell he lacks the ideological assurance required for the traditional poetry of mores, and he evades the responsibility by writing occasional verse instead. But Prior's version of the mode is a specific enactment of the scepticism and wit of the Restoration court poets as well as of their stylishness and fashionable ease.

"Wit Grows Polite"

Prior's version of the court wits is nevertheless a specifically polite and modern one. He reflects in this his own social distance from them as aristocrats or wealthy court gentry as well as the general cultural changes of the period. He insists, for example, that the conversational wit to which he certainly attaches a great importance must be polite:

> Poet Bays said of his Rant, if it is not civil egad it must be sublime; but in ordinary Conversation it is a very low Character to be as witty as you can, many like the thing, but few esteem the Person, and if a Man is thought to have so much Wit, that his good Nature begins to be called in Question, in my Opinion he has made but a sad bargain by the Exchange. (1, 584–86)

The note of disillusionment he strikes has a distinctly Restoration quality at times, "Who would, says Dryden, Drink this draught of Life?" (1, 159). But Prior does not show the full bitterness of the court wits. He is more truly secular rather than irreligious and blasphemous like Rochester.

In one group of songs that includes the clever poem on adultery "Since we your Husband daily see" Prior displays, as his editors point out, a marked Restoration quality.[8] A libertine or at least naturalist tone is apparent, and a frank sexual gratitude. Yet even these poems are relatively mild, a matter of witty sexual metaphor, a blend of euphemism and audacity rather than explicit detail. He seems almost entirely to lack that sense of sin on which the more shocking modes of the court wits depend for their effect. "Chloe Beauty has and Wit" shows the characteristic tone of decorous obscenity:

> And 'twould be a cruel thing
> When her black Eyes have rais'd desire,
> Shou'd she not her Bucket bring
> And kindly help to quench the Fire.

> (1, 715)

In the later poem "The Dove" we see the full metamorphosis into a specifically eighteenth-century kind of eroticism. The whole tone is so elaborately polite and the final sexual reference so oblique that it seems at first as if Prior is refining it out of existence. In reality, of course, the paraphernalia of the poem and its coyness actually serve to draw attention to its conclusion. The details of London social life, with references to St. Dunstan's clock, footmen on a visiting day, and the teapot combine with delicately conventional rural imagery, elegant love compliment, the playful mythological finery of Cupid and Venus, and decorous obscenity to make a poem that has something of the atmosphere of a Fragonard painting:

> O, whither do those Fingers rove,
> Cries CHLOE, treacherous Urchin, whither?
> O VENUS! I shall find thy DOVE,
> Says He; for sure I touch his Feather.
>
> (121–24, 1, 437)

The well-known "An English Padlock" takes up the sexual cynicism of Ovid and of Wycherley's *The Country Wife*. But it does so only to alter it almost beyond recognition, for the real moral of the poem comes instead with the emotional weight of the last few lines—tender, domestic, but patronizing and rather unromantic, the tone most characteristic of the love lyrics:

> And when these certain Ills to shun
> She would to Thy Embraces run;
> Receive Her with extended Arms:
> Seem more delighted with her Charms:
> Wait on Her to the Park and Play:
> Put on good Humour, make Her gay;
> Be to her Virtues very kind:
> Be to her Faults a little blind:
> Let all her Ways be unconfin'd:
> And clap your PADLOCK—on her Mind.
>
> (72–83, 1, 229)

Prior has moved beyond the open Restoration misogyny, and writes fewer direct satires on women than most poets of the period. But the new feeling he cultivates obviously has its patronising side—a tendency presumably accentuated by his well-known propensity for women regarded as beneath the social status to which he had attained. He calls his mistress "child," for example, and makes a point of explaining his classical allusion, "the God of us Verse-men (You know Child) the Sun" ("A Better Answer," 1, 450). "An English Padlock" is very clear in the way it softens traditional patriarchal controls yet at the same time tries to internalize them by sentiment.

This new sentiment reflects the decline of the old courtly Petrarchan imagery and the new movement toward "affective individualism" and the cultivation of passive feminine virtues. Prior's own polite sentiment mediates between aristocratic wit and the new complexes of feeling. His typical tone has an almost domestic quality, and he resolutely refuses the imagery of transcendence. One stanza of "A Better Answer," for example, is analogous to Rochester's:

> When wearied with a world of Woe,
> To thy safe Bosom I retire
> Where Love, and Peace, and Truth does flow,
> May I contented there expire,
> Lest once more wandring from that Heav'n
> I fall on some base heart unblest:
> Faithless to thee, False, unforgiv'n
> And lose my Everlasting rest.[9]

Prior's version is much cosier in tone:

> So when I am weary'd with wand'ring all Day;
> To Thee my Delight in the Evening I come:
> No Matter what Beauties I saw in my Way:
> They were but my Visits; but Thou art my Home.
>
> (21–24)

The anapestic rhythm is obviously jauntier and much less intense than Rochester's movement to a dramatic climax. The range of reference has been amazingly narrowed down and domesticated, and eighteenth-century social visits replace sin and damnation.

Prior's Poise

Prior's occasional mode represents a withdrawal from politics and public solemnity into private life and relaxation. If he is distanced from the fullness of the old ideology in his Restoration scepticism, so is he from the fullness of the new. Although politically close to Swift, he does not live to see what the latter regarded as the full development of the new society, and he makes few direct or convincing attacks on the new ethos. But in his disillusionment with politics and his Restoration dislike of false sublimity he is distanced from the spirit of Whig pan-

egyrical poetry after the earliest phases of his career. His privileging of leisure also sets him at odds with the new ethos, although,
like Parnell's this sense of leisure is itself a diminished one. Even
more markedly than the rest of these poets Prior in fact reveals a
split between the sense that poetry is less serious than prose and
"business" of various kinds and the feeling that poetry is leisured, stylish, and upper-class and thus superior to business.

"Written in the Year 1696," for example, combines a strong
sense of public image with a commensurate delight in slipping
the reins of the public world. Prior goes home "In a little Dutch
chaise on a Saturday night," with his volume of Horace in one
hand, his mistress's hand in the other. Love and poetry are both
the realm of leisure:

> While with Labour Assiduous due pleasure I mix
> And in one day attone for the Busyness of Six

They are to that extent both marginalized against a workaday
world that is the main one, and Prior is concerned not with
sexual guilt, but with the need to justify taking a holiday, "Since
none can with Justice my pleasures oppose." At the same time
there is an obvious sense of hedonistic triumph in the poem that
is related to a social disdain for bourgeois Holland, "In *Holland*
half drownded in Interest and Prose."

The poem is polished in its classical allusions, which are
clearly part of the definition of stylishness. For Prior, although a
member of the ancients' party in this keen classicism, is modern
in spirit in many respects too and concerned to be relevant. As he
says in his "Heads for a Treatise upon Learning":

> Again the Customes and Maximes of the Greeks and Romans are so
> different from those of the present Nations and times that thô we may
> be thought more learned we are not in proportion so fully instructed
> from these. (1, 580–81)

"Written in the year 1696" is thus very representative in its self-
consciously modern celebration of the present combined with
genuine respect and even nostalgia for the classical past:

> So with *Phia* thrô *Athens Pisistratus* rode
> Men thought her *Minerva* and Him a new God
> But why shou'd I stories of Athens rehearse
> Where People knew Love and were partial to Verse
> Since none can with Justice my pleasures oppose

In *Holland* half drownded in Interest and Prose:
By *Greece* and past Ages what need I be try'd
When the *Hague* and the Present are both on my side
And is it enough for the Joys of the day
To think what *Anacreon* or *Sapho* wou'd say
When good *Vandergoos* and his provident Vrough
As they gaze on my triumph do freely allow
That search all the province, you'l find no Man there is
So blest as the *Englischen Heer* SECRETARIS.

(1, 158)

Like Gay's *Trivia* this is neither mock-heroic nor heroic, but a humorous recognition of the genuine pleasures of the modern world combined with a certain sense of regret about modern demystification in contrast to a time when "People knew Love and were partial to Verse." But Prior's is presented as a personal synthesis, with perhaps some exemplary dimensions to it. Gay on the other hand is making a statement about modern culture as a whole. Prior does not even pretend to incorporate the full realities of the present, which are relegated in a half-intimidated, half-dismissive way to prose.

Yet the poem's balance is impressive, and its self-portrait highly attractive. Prior combines in characteristic fashion rakish hedonism, genuine love sentiment, and a touch of Horatian stoicism: "This Night and the next shal be Hers shal be Mine, / To good or ill Fortune the Third we resign." He has developed a distinctively eighteenth-century version of the style and tradition of the Restoration court wits, strengthened by an urbane detachment and tolerance modeled on Horace and Montaigne. He reflects a modern feeling of demystification and yet provides a partial defence against loss. A wry sense of the place of convention, and an acceptance of limited, realistic goals are part of Prior's highly deliberate self-presentation. As he puts it elsewhere:

Yet counting as far as to Fifty his years
His Virtues and Vices were as other mens are,
High Hopes he conceiv'd, and he smother'd great fears,
In a Life party-coloured, half pleasure, half care.

("For his own Epitaph," 1, 409)

The best group of love poems—"On Beauty," "The Question, To Lisetta," "Lisetta's Reply," "The Garland," "The Lady who offers her Looking Glass to Venus," "Chloe Jealous," "Answer to

Chloe Jealous, in the same Stile. The Author sick," and "A Better
Answer"—strongly highlight the "Diff'rence there is betwixt
Nature and Art." Demystification verges at times on disillusionment, but Prior avoids not only the cosmic imagery of Rochester
but also the profound bitterness of his disappointment. For love
is not the place to look for transcendent satisfactions anyway.
Like the poet-hero in Sidney's *Astrophel and Stella*, Prior is torn
between love and public life, but Prior is more genuinely disillusioned about what he gives up than the Elizabethan poet as well
as far less idealistic about love:

> Ambition, Business, Friendship, News,
> My useful Books, and serious Muse,
> For THIS I willingly decline
> The Mirth of Feasts, and Joys of Wine;
> And chuse to sit and talk with Thee
> (As Thy great Orders may decree)
> Of Cocks and Bulls, of Flutes and Fiddles,
> Of Idle Tales and foolish Riddles.

("On Beauty, A Riddle," 1, 445)

The tone is a teasing one, but women are ultimately seen as
incapable of serious conversation, and the "Serious muse" and
love poetry are no longer compatible.

It is the implicit privileging of convention itself that emerges
as one of the most significant themes of the group. If the domes-
ticity, tenderness, and honesty of these poems reflect what have
been regarded as the bourgeois influence of "affective individualism," Prior still opposes any idea of pure sincerity. He has a
sophisticated awareness of artifice and social pressure and a
sense, tinged with sadness, of their unavoidability: "Let us e'en
talk a little like folk of this world." "Sincerity" is thus a complex
phenomenon, for "A Better Answer" is a love poem claiming to
be sincere by saying that poetry is unreal, and rejecting convention at the same time as it keeps the imagery of Venus and
references to tradition:

> Then finish, dear CHLOE, this Pastoral War;
> And let us like HORACE and LYDIA agree:
> For Thou art a girl as much brighter than Her,
> As he was a Poet sublimer than Me.[10]

The same sense of the pressures of convention and the social
world is present in all Prior's work. The increased social inter-

mingling, the movement away from behavior based on rural or court rules, and the growth of London all contributed to the sense of a possible disjunction between public and private selves in the period, as well as to the awareness of acting a role. Like Swift in "Verses on the Death of Dr. Swift," Prior exploits the coffee-house motif, in, for example, "The Conversation. A Tale," where he hears an account of his politics and poetry from a complete stranger who claims to be a close friend. Prior is to some degree wary of the benefits of the new public sphere. The poem conveys a sophisticated sense of his own public image as well as illustrating the difficulties caused by increased social mixing among people previously unknown to each other:

> It always has been thought discreet,
> To know the Company You meet;
> And sure there may be secret Danger,
> In talking much before a Stranger.
>
> (1–4, 1, 523)

"An English Padlock" includes what purports to be satire of the *beau monde:*

> Send Her abroad: and let Her see,
> That all this mingled Mass, which She,
> Being forbidden, longs to know,
> Is a dull Farce, an empty show,
> Powder, and Pocket-Glass, and Beau;
> A Staple of Romance and Lies,
> False Tears, and real Perjuries:
> Where Sighs and Looks are bought and sold;
> And Love is made but to be told:
> Where the fat Bawd, and lavish Heir
> The spoils of ruin'd Beauty share.
>
> (1, 228)

The disillusionment here no doubt real enough, but the satiric bitterness is merely rhetorical. This is the cynicism characteristic of a man who knows the way of the world and takes it for granted. He expects no moral or social transformation.

For if the demystification of convention reveals disillusionment, it is convention itself that provides a stay against it. Prior's very real pessimism and melancholy is not allowed to take itself too seriously. The sadness of life is balanced by the gentleman's real pleasures and by a tolerant acceptance of our need for illusions even as we recognize that they are illusions. "To the Honourable Charles Montagu" (1, 108–9), for example, leads inevitably to the implication that Prior and Montagu *are* deceiving themselves in both the public ambition suitable to the aristocrat Montagu and the private affection suitable to Prior:

> We weary'd should lye down in Death,
> This cheat of Life would take no more;
> If you thought Fame but empty Breath,
> I, PHILLIS but a perjur'd Whore.

Nevertheless we have to accept illusions in order to keep on living:

> If We see right We see our Woes:
> Then what avails it to have Eyes?
> From Ignorance our Comfort flows:
> The only Wretched are the Wise.

It is *Alma* that represents the greatest triumph of this mode. The poem is a friendly conversation and debate, the epitome of coffee-house philosophy. It carries lightly an immense range of reference and a great freight of unsystematic learning, popularizing it effectively yet at the same time setting experience against authority, so that the period's distrust for abstract reasoning is incorporated too. For the poem is sceptical in import,[11] showing how the mind is governed by the body and how small a part reason plays in our actions and opinions.

Prior's colloquial diction and his meter are therefore of the highest appropriateness. Borrowed from Butler, they are nevertheless politer than their original—racy and disillusioned, but without bitterness, although certainly set in deliberate contrast to more "poetic" meters and to "Poetic Madness" (1, 411). The style is especially appropriate for Prior's brief burlesques of the classics:

> In scornful Sloth ACHILLES slept;
> And for his Wench, like TALL-BOY, wept:
> Nor would return to War and Slaughter;
> 'Till they brought back the Parson's Daughter.

(1, 483–86)

The meter carries a similar charge in the revealing passage of scepticism about traditional love images:

> That CUPID goes with Bow and Arrows,
> And VENUS keeps her Coach and Sparrows,
> Is all but Emblem, to acquaint One,
> The Son is sharp, the Mother wanton.
> Such images have sometimes shown,
> A *Mystic* Sense, but oft'ner None.
> For who conceives, what Bards devise,
> That Heav'n is plac'd in *Celia's* Eyes?
> Or where's the Sense, direct or moral,
> That Teeth are Pearl, or Lips are Coral.
>
> (1, 389–98)

In Canto 2 Prior discusses the manners of different societies in a way that expresses the relativism inherent in theories of "civility." He makes humorous links between decorum in dress and poetry (2, 31–44) and is concerned to present normative patterns of behavior himself by satirising, for example, the antiquarian collectors and virtuosi. Still, the satire is far from virulent, and there is no moral indignation:

> Now, ALMA, to Divines and Prose
> I leave thy Frauds, and Crimes and Woes:
> Nor think To-night of Thy Ill-Nature,
> But of Thy Follies, Idle Creature,
> The turns of Thy uncertain Wing,
> And not the Malice of Thy Sting.
>
> (3, 472–77)

The suggestion is that Prior's kind of poetry is less serious than prose, but more diverting, and that *Alma* is secular rather than theological. The expression of human absurdities reveals an amused tolerance, as in the picture of "old MADGE, bewitch'd at Sixty one," who still loves dancing and "cheats her Son, to wed her Page" (2, 319; 334).

Scepticism and melancholy are real enough in *Alma*, but they are transcended by the special poise of the poem between Matt's views and Richard's pragmatism:

> Tir'd with these Thoughts—Less tir'd than I
> Quoth Dick, with Your Philosophy—
> That People live and dye, I knew
> An hour ago, as well as You.
> And if Fate spin Us longer Years,
> Or is in haste to take the Shears;
> I know, We must Both Fortunes try,

> And bear our Evils, wet or dry.
> Yet let the Goddess smile, or frown;
> Bread We shall eat, or white or brown:
> And in a Cottage, or a Court,
> Drink fine *Champaigne*, or muddl'd *Port*.

(3, 578–88)

The self-depreciating dismissal of the moral truisms of the rest of the poem attractively sets experience against books, and the rhythms are strengthened by fortitude. Dick stands at a distance from both the public and the private myths of the period, the court and the cottage; and the content of his antitheses is down-to-earth and worldly. "Bread we shall eat, or white or brown . . . fine *Champaigne*, or muddl'd *Port*." The goddess Fortune herself has more than a purely literary weight behind her. She is defied, but nothing is done to make the Horatian solidity of the close Christian. We move, as at the end of "To Charles Montagu," although with less devastating effect, into a sense of the need for illusions to help us carry on living:

> And must We Spectacles apply,
> To view, what hurts our naked Eye?
>
> . . . .
>
> If to be sad is to be wise;
> I do most heartily despise
> Whatever SOCRATES has said,
> Or TULLY writ, or WANLEY read.

(3, 592–93; 606–9)

The modern word "poise" is perhaps the closest approximation to the quality Prior recommends, but that conveys only a small part of its great ideological centrality in his ethos. Polite stylishness and a modified form of Restoration wit—versions of *sprezzatura*—retain all the gloss of social glamor, but they are expanded into something that cannot easily be defined or pinned down:

> BEYOND the fix'd and settl'd Rules
> Of Vice and Virtue in the Schools,
> Beyond the Letter of the Law,
> Which keeps our Men and Maids in Awe,
> The better Sort should set before 'em
> A Grace, a Manner, a Decorum;
> Something that gives their Acts a Light;
> Makes 'em not only just, but bright;

And sets 'em in that open Fame,
Which witty Malice cannot blame.

("Paulo Purganti," 1–10, 1, 260)

The wonderfully relaxed expression of this is part of its very definition. What Prior is referring to is not a moral quality as such, for it is beyond the rules of vice or virtue. Yet it includes morality ("not only just"). It requires a social consensus, "that open Fame," and yet has an intrinsic quality as well. If it is a kind of grace, the religious analogy has no real substance to it. The phrase "the better Sort" obviously has class connotations as well as moral ones, but they are left as vague as possible.

What Prior wishes to present us with in his polite occasional verse is a personal achievement that includes sophistication, intelligence, and humor, and that confronts pessimism with urbane courage. But this is an ideologically validated exemplary quality as well. It carries over a quasi-aristocratic superiority without its traditional ideological supports and attempts to reconcile the best of the past with a genuine modernity, although from a personal rather than a fully cultural perspective. Prior propounds at the same time a businesslike realism and a stylish disdain for the mundane realities of business, and he successfully evades many of the resulting contradictions. He exemplifies "A Grace, a Manner, a Decorum" that is a way of coming to terms with the disillusionments and demystifications of the period, but that also has a very rich mystique reconferred upon it.

John Gay's "Due Civilities": The Ironies of Politeness

Polite Evasiveness

Manners fascinate Gay. His work is full of the minutiae and technical terms of fashion, but he also has a strong sense of manners in the much deeper sense of mores, the customary behavior and lifestyles of the different levels of a traditionally stratified social system. He delights to parallel and invert the manners of high and low. As the beggar says of Gay's greatest success:

> Through the whole Piece you may observe such a similitude of Manners in high and low Life that it is difficult to determine whether (in the fashionable Vices) the fine Gentlemen imitate the Gentlemen of the Road, or the Gentlemen of the Road the fine Gentlemen.[1]

Through his pages parade beaux and society ladies, shepherds and criminals, whose manners mimic each other in rich and ironic ways.

Such devices of paralleling and inversion are themselves traditional, and they are conservative rather than radical in implication. They suggest a failure in the upper classes to live up to their responsibility of setting a good example, and this is usually their final effect in Gay too. He seeks to reimpose the old pattern of mores on the bewildering new politeness. Yet Gay's own work also reflects the slide from mores to politeness. The pattern of inversions in Gay is so insistent that, despite its basically conservative intention, it also seems to reflect genuine questions about whether social distinctions are natural or artificial. Gay can identify completely neither with the older nor with the newer ideologies. Like Pope and Swift rather than Parnell and Prior, he is ambitious enough to try to provide a cultural evaluation of modern politeness as a whole. What is especially characteristic of his work, however, is the way that both his old-fashioned, quasi-feudal critique of eighteenth-century politeness and his more modern questioning are dissolved into a form of pastoral sentiment. His cultivation of popular elements and his descriptions of the poor seem to criticise eighteenth-century politeness. But the softening of such elements into charm is Gay's own version of polite consensus.

In "A Letter to a Lady, Occasion'd by the Arrival of Her Royal Highness The Princess of Wales" (1714) Gay refers humorously to the situation of the true laureate poet:

> Had *Virgil* ne'er at Court improv'd his Strains,
> He still had sung of Flocks and homely Swains;
> And had not *Horace* sweet Preferment found,
> The *Roman* Lyre had never learnt to sound.[2]

His case is that, if he received the proper financial support for a laureate poet, he could produce laureate verse. Of course, Gay has his tongue in his cheek in emphasising the finances of the laureate role. What he does produce in this poem is a charming compliment to the royal family that is actually the closer to being successful laureate verse for incorporating a recognition of the virtual impossibility of the mode in contemporary circum-stances. The poem is both a serious and a nonserious "laureate" poem and a serious and a nonserious request for money.

Even as late as 1727 in the first volume of the *Fables*, Gay produces a curiously diminished version of the laureate mode in addressing these poems to Prince William and thus purporting to be guiding his moral education. But it is not only the lack of patronage that makes full-scale laureate verse impossible now, as Gay really proves in his pretense at writing high flights in the earlier poem. For the change in patterns of patronage is also a change in ideology. This royal family no longer needs poets, and to apply to them the old pattern of mythology and idealization would truly be ridiculous. For all the respect and religious obe-dience still accorded kings, the world of politics is now a much more secularized one. As Gay writes elsewhere:

> Where news and politicks divide mankind,
> And schemes of state involve th'uneasie mind;
> Faction embroils the world; and ev'ry tongue
> Is mov'd by flatt'ry, or with scandal hung:
> Friendship, for sylvan shades, the palace flies,
> Where all must yield to int'rest's dearer ties;

Each rival *Machiavel* with envy burns,
And honesty forsakes them all by turns;
While calumny upon each party's thrown,
Which both promote, and both alike disown.

(*Rural Sports* 13–22, vol. 1, p. 42)

These are impressive and heartfelt lines from a not very impressive poem. Like Parnell, Prior, Swift, and Pope, Gay laments
the rise of the party system. Even if he were to obtain financial
patronage from such a world, how could a poet draw from it the
authority to write properly on mores?

Gay was actually far more dependent on specific court and
aristocratic patronage than Pope. At the same time he made more
money from the sale of his poetry than Parnell or Prior, not to
mention the success of his plays. Gay can only be called a semi-
professional. He made his living through the combination of a
small private income, receipts from the plays and poems, sub-
scriptions, and aristocratic and court patronage. He uses the title
Poems on Several Occasions to assimilate his work to the amateur tradition because full patronage is not available either from
the traditional sources or from the market and because he has an
unresolved conflict about the poet's relationship to commercialism.[3]

The tone of wit and *sprezzatura* is also attractive to Gay in
itself. It is an assertion of his own stylishness. He submits *Three
Hours after Marriage* to all "who think Good-Breeding is a-kin to
Wit."[4] But the tone is a matter of temperament as well. Like Prior,
Gay would have been temperamentally indisposed to write in the
full tradition of laureate verse even if the patronage had been
available and the cultural climate more inviting. He is very much
a poet of the party of wit. He writes a few poems like "A Con-
templation on Night" and "A Thought on Eternity" in the vein of
Protestant moralizing and high seriousness. But his own most
typical work is inveterately secular. He displays the characteristic courtly disdain for solemn moralizing:

What gain we by this solemn way of teaching?
Our precepts mend your lives no more than Preaching.[5]

His nonchalance and scepticism reveal a clear aristocratic and
Restoration court bias:

Life is a jest and all things show it;
I thought so once, but now I know it.

("My own Epitaph," 1, 253)

It is appropriate therefore that, though Gay's career shows a self-conscious commitment to poetry, he never makes the claims that a full-time poet might make. He writes half-seriously, half-humorously to Pope, "For my part, who do not deal in Heroes or ravish'd Ladys, I may perhaps celebrate a milkmaid, describe the amours of your Parson's Daughter, or write an Elegy upon the death of a Hare."[6] In fact his most typical form is the poem in two or three short books, intermediate in length between the long forms of the full-time poet and the short forms of the occasional amateur. Such modes evade the full seriousness of the older laureate mode and its commentary on mores. They also distance Gay from the expansive sublimity of Whig panegyrical poetry. "Wine" is significant here. No criticism of Milton is, of course, intended. Yet the diminution of epic seriousness is symptomatic of one aspect of "wit," a defensive reaction against something that these poets could neither attain successfully themselves nor directly mock and dismiss, as they could Milton's successors.

Gay's lighthearted *sprezzatura* and wit, his quasi-aristocratic stylishness, is a part of his politeness, but it is complicated by a strong, old-fashioned, gentry sense of social justice and the place of the poor. He was himself from a minor landed gentry family and was brought up in a small town in Devon. This background obviously contributes to the way Gay resists the frigid divorce between polite and plebeian culture. Robert Malcolmson reminds us that not all gentlemen of the period felt entirely "disengaged from the culture of the common people. They frequently occupied something of a half-way house between the robust, unpolished culture of provincial England and the cosmopolitan, sophisticated culture which was based in London."[7] Only in *The Beggar's Opera*, however, does any of this amount to a real attack on eighteenth-century politeness. The use of popular elements and the reminders about the poor enter into strange alliances with artificiality and polite sentiment.

For if Gay often questions modern politeness he has no clear alternative set of norms from the past to offer either. He shares many of the sympathies of Swift and Pope, but his attitude is not consistently and unambiguously a Tory one. His most Tory work, apart from the heavy-handed and derivative second volume of *The Fables*, is *The What D'Ye Call it*, where real indignation is expressed about the injustices perpetrated on the rustics of the play by those who are supposed to be their protectors. In the end social justice is won by the dramatic trick of the play within the play that turns out not to have been a play. Here, as in *The*

Beggar's Opera, a hall of mirrors is set up that is both brilliant and bewildering. A Tory norm for the countryside is ultimately reestablished, but a real ambivalence remains. The fact that justice and order can be brought about only by a trick implies that they are normally absent. On the other hand there is a blunting of indignation since no harm is actually done in the end. Like *The Beggar's Opera,* the play insistently raises questions about the relationship between drama and real life, but it makes no attempt to answer them. The final effect combines deep regret for the loss of Tory order with a denial of seriousness and a distancing that implies at the same time the outdatedness, even the irrelevance, of the ideal.

In his pamphlet *The Present State of Wit* (London, 1711), Gay warmly praises Addison and Steele. Like them he attacks decadent Restoration ideas of what was gentlemanly and argues that true politeness must include moral respectability:

> It would have been a jest sometime since, for a man to have asserted, that any thing witty could be said in praise of a Marry'd State, or that Devotion and Virtue were any way necessary to the Character of a fine Gentleman.[8]

Clearly there is an overlap here between the ethos of the *Spectator* writers and Gay's gentry moralism. But this element conflicts with the antimoralistic note of *sprezzatura,* especially in its Restoration versions. He is much more secular than Addison and Steele and much less moralistic overall. He condemns upper-class idleness and constantly praises work, but his wish to make it a central value is often defeated by the remnants of his own quasi-aristocratic prejudices. As well as the characteristic split between aristocratic and middling-gentry values, he shares the typical ambivalence of the minor landed gentry about the development of a commercial society. As was not uncommon in declining gentry families, he had himself been apprenticed for several years to a silk merchant in London. He praises merchants and commerce warmly at times. In the last decade of his life he especially supports Bolingbroke's campaign to show that Walpole's foreign policy was against the interests of British trade. But his landed bias and aristocratic prejudices distance him from the commercial and urban ethos of *The Spectator.* Influenced by Swift and Pope, he grows more and more disaffected with the corruptions of a commercial society.

Not fully committed to any of the main ideological traditions,

Gay lacks the authority for the most serious modes of commentary on mores and politeness. He evades the longer forms of epic or Whig panegyrical poetry, but he also lacks the authority of the true satirist. The politeness of Gay involves a softening of the different strands of critique that his work certainly contains. In part perhaps, this was because of the need for patronage. He writes in the prologue to *The Captives*:

> He shows most wit who gives the most offence,
> But still our squeamish author satyr loathes.

Despite the success of *The Beggar's Opera* he was actually, said Pope,

> remarkable for an unwillingness to offend the great, by any of his writings. He had an uncommon timidity upon him in relation to any thing of that sort. And yet you see what ill luck he had that way after all his care not to offend![9]

No totally consistent class ethos or even ethical position emerges in fact in Gay's work. He attacks the *"Genteel Mania"* of social climbing, sarcastically making a cit's wife say to her husband, "Sure 'tis fitting that your wife / Shou'd copy ladies of the court."[10] He criticizes the *nouveaux riches* and "the griping Broker" in *Trivia*. A coxcomb, "vain of his unknown Race" (2, 577) has replaced the true aristocracy, whose great London houses have regrettably been lost. But there is some collusion on Gay's part in what conservative writers see as these reprehensible and threatening results of the growing consumerism. His enjoyment of all the aberrant phenomena he describes is often evident. It is often difficult to be certain of Gay's tone or to know which of his contradictions are deliberate. In a well-known case from *Trivia* the "Walker" praises oysters and recommends his readers to stop and enjoy some, but then moves into a condemnation of the "Luxury" that will ransack "Earth, Sea and Air" for its pleasures (3. 185–204, vol. 1, 165–66). The mock-heroic tone may take the force from the attack, but it does not remove the contradiction, which has been seen by one commentator as part of a full-scale satiric portrayal of a deluded persona.[11] Yet this contradiction between moralistic condemnation and enjoyment of the effects of luxury and commercialism is frequent in Gay's work, even when he is clearly writing as himself.

In "The Fan," for example, which reached two editions in 1714, the intention is obviously mildly satiric. To focus attention

to such a degree on fans is to produce a *reductio ad absurdum* of
the trivial interests of the world of fashion. On the other hand, to
attribute to the gods the creation of the fashionable appurte-
nances of "the fair" is also to pay women an elaborate compliment. The whole poem is so mythological and airy that the
element of satire on the *beau monde* becomes no more than
conventional, and Gay himself testifies to the danger:

> Should you the Wardrobe's Magazine rehearse,
> And glossy Manteaus rustle in thy Verse;
> Should you the rich Brocaded Suit unfold,
> Where rising Flow'rs grow stiff with frosted Gold;
> The dazled Muse would from her Subject stray,
> And in a Maze of Fashions lose her Way.
>
> (2. 239–44, vol. 1, p. 65–66)

The Rape of the Lock is able to express the same ambivalent
fascination without destroying the satire. Gay's uncertainty is
especially revealed in his tinkering with the ending. The 1713
version ends satirically. Corinna receives from Strephon the gift
for which he has begged the gods, but she uses it only to express
her preference for a fop:

> The gay coquette, of her last Conquest vain,
> Snatches the Trinket from the trembling Swain,
> Then turns around with a disdainful Mien,
> Smiles on the Fop, and flirts the new Machine.
>
> (3. 195–98, vol. 1, p. 79)

By the time of the 1720 edition, however, Gay has moved toward
the new emphasis on sentiment and moralism; Corinna learns
from the moral examples on the fan, realizes her "Strephon's
Constancy sincere" (3. 202), and they marry.

Gay is unable satisfactorily to distinguish true politeness from
false or to decide what criteria for evaluation to use. "The Epistle
to William Pulteney," for example, is in part a brilliant definition
of the false politeness with which Gay's French interlocutor is
predictably delighted:

> Pardon me, Sir; we know the *Paris* mode,
> And gather *Politesse* from Courts abroad.
> Like you, our Courtiers keep a num'rous train
> To load their coach; and tradesmen dun in vain.
> Nor has Religion left us in the lurch,
> And, as in *France*, our vulgar croud the Church;

Our Ladys too support the Masquerade,
The sex by nature love th'intriguing trade.
Straight the vain fop in ign'rant rapture crys,
Paris *the barb'rous world will civilize!*

(151–60, vol. 1, p. 212)

But Gay's descriptions are full of enjoyment of the decadently fashionable French scene, and he well recognizes his own collusion:

Yes, I can sagely, when the times are past,
Laugh at those follys which I strove to taste.

(3–4, vol. 1, p. 208)

More importantly he is too confused about what he wants to say about Britain and British politeness to carry through the traditional distinction between the manly and honest manners of the English and the decadence and effeminacy of the French.[12] He creates the expectation that the moral organization of the poem is to be on that model and then disappoints it. For in fact the English are just as bad:

Like a Court Lady though he write and spell,
His minuet step was fashion'd by *Marcell;*
He dresses, fences. What avails to know?
For women chuse their men, like silks, for show.
Is this the thing, you cry, that *Paris* boasts?
Is this the thing renown'd among our Toasts?
For such a flutt'ring sight we need not roam;
Our own Assemblys shine with these at home.

(57–64, vol. 1, p. 209)

One brilliant and well-known passage describes how Londoners make for the open air when spring comes,

When the sweet-breathing spring unfolds the buds,
Love flies the dusty town for shady woods.
Then *Totenham* fields with roving beauty swarm,
And *Hampstead* Balls the city virgin warm.

(101–4, vol. 1, p. 210)

Gay gives us a version of the conventional idea in the suggestion that this is only a "cit" phenomenon in England, whereas in Paris,

even Court Ladies sin in open air.
. . . here no wife can blast her husbands fame,
Cuckold is grown an honourable name.

                                                    (109, 113–14)

Yet he confers a genuine mock-pastoral beauty on the activities of
his cits, such as to undermine the social satire to a considerable
degree. Furthermore, he goes on to say that in Charles II's time the
English upper classes behaved just as the French and the cits do
now:

Such were our pleasures in the days of yore,
When am'rous *Charles Britannia's* scepter bore;
Then nightly scene of joy the *Park* was made,
And Love in couples peopled ev'ry shade.

                                                    (127–30)

Gentry moralism against the decadent Restoration upper
classes is obviously present here, although the tone makes it hard
to detect much satiric force behind the passage. But the logic of
the whole satiric scheme is subverted when he cannot resist
pointing out that in modern English court circles the same activities simply take place indoors. Contemporary English courtiers are not more moral but simply more hypocritical than both
the cits and their own upper-class counterparts at the Restoration
and in contemporary France:

But since at Court the rural taste is lost,
What mighty summs have velvet couches cost!

                                                    (131–32)

The worldly cynicism is highly amusing, but it takes away any
moral vantage point. For Gay is not consistently subverting a
complacent cliché to embarrass his own countrymen. He tries to re-
establish the manly-free-Britain-versus-decadent-enslaved-
France antithesis again at the end in a way that can hardly
convince us after what has gone before.[13]

The Shepherd's Week and Trivia

Gay's two most attractive poems, The Shepherd's Week and
Trivia, may, in juxtaposing town and country manners, be said to

raise the question of the naturalness of modern politeness. But they do so only with the greatest obliqueness, and it is partly because their evasiveness is much more subtle and complex that they are more successful poetically. They are traditionalist and "polite" poems at the same time, split between old and new both formally and in their values. Gay juxtaposes the new ethos and the old ideology, but his faith in the old mores is enough to prevent a full enthusiasm for the new politeness without being enough to provide any real alternative. He colludes with his polite readers himself in other respects. These poems create the expectation and appearance of ideological evaluation and choice, but they do so only to elude it. The manners of Gay's shepherds, for example, are completely spontaneous and indivisible from the mores appropriate to their lifestyle and station. In presenting this reminder of the presence of the poor, this image of one part at least of traditional rural order, and these robust popular elements, Gay faces his readers with realities that polite poetry normally ignores and may thus be thought to be providing a critique of the limitations of eighteenth-century politeness. But the poem has long been recognised to be a deeply ambiguous achievement. His shepherds can hardly be thought of as providing a full set of alternative norms to the polite world. In its very pastoral quality *The Shepherd's Week* softens its critique into sentiment, and the poem confirms polite prejudices at the same time as it challenges them.

In William Empson's brilliant analysis of traditional pastoral, he established that it depends on the old aristocratic ideological complex that implies a link between the highest and lowest social levels, a beautiful harmony between rich and poor. It incorporates the idea that the poor are ultimately the same as the nobly born, but in a reassuring rather than a radical way.[14] It includes Christian attitudes about the special status of the lowly and humble, but softens them into beautiful sentiment. It also implies an aristocratic perspective in its distancing from labor.

The relationship between literary convention and social reality is never, of course, a direct one, but the rise of politeness made all these fictions harder to sustain. As social status became more flexible, it also ceased to be an unassailably secure matter, and there was thus a greater need to assert differentiation from the vulgar. As a consequence, traditional pastoral came to seem more artificial in its attribution of beautiful feelings to them.[15] The portrayal of shepherds as idle also came to seem awkward as

aristocratic traditions of leisure became less central. The conventions of the old version of pastoral were ceasing to have any
vitalizing relationship with ideology at all.

In setting out to parody the strategy of realism that some poets
developed as an attempt to save pastoral, Gay finds a way of
preserving a genuine pastoral note himself, as all commentators
have testified.[16] Instead of the milkmaid from *Rural Sports* who
"rich in poverty, enjoys content" (2, 413, vol. 1, p. 57), we have
shepherds who are innocent in a different sense through their
relatively innocuous naughtiness. Gay has replaced the idealism
of the old pastoral with a curious and characteristic blend of
cynicism and sentiment. He contrives to appear to avoid senti-
mentality and artificiality, but in reality, as John Barrell wittily
writes, he presents only a more complex form of it:

> The countryside of England was henceforth considered to be popu-
> lated by desirable girls, who, though they might be hoped to dis-
> tribute their favours with some freedom, did so with a bashful
> sincerity which added to their charm; and by honest clowns, who
> were incapable of fine feelings but who knew, at least, how to have a
> good time, and were likely to devote the same rough energy to their
> work as to their play.[17]

The sense we gain of the emotional limitations of these shepherds is humorous but patronizing:

> Thus wail'd the Louts, in melancholy strain,
> 'Till bonny *Susan* sped a-cross the Plain;
> They seiz'd the Lass in Apron clean array'd,
> And to the Ale-house forc'd the willing Maid;
> In Ale and Kisses they forget their Cares,
> And *Susan Blouzelinda's* Loss repairs.
>
>   ("Friday," 159–64)

Gay forces his polite readers to ask themselves whether they are
more sensitive than the shepherds are or simply more hypocritical. But the comic note takes any real critical force from the
latter suggestion, too. A kind of hypocrisy, Gay implies, is a part
of the sophistication of politeness. All politeness, as Empson
says, has an element of irony about it.[18] Gay's readers are encouraged into the double enjoyment of a poignant nostalgia for the
uncomplicated lives of the rustics and a sense of the burden and
the privilege of their own sophistication.

To reactivate pastoral is in one sense to criticise the new

ideology that had made the genre problematic. On the other hand, to suggest it is still possible despite the changed circumstances is to be reassuring. The old pastoral emphasis on innocence as superior to social rank attains a more genuinely critical edge after the breakup of the ideology that had been able to incorporate it into an elaborate system.[19] But if Gay voices criticism he also softens it by reintroducing pastoral sentiment. Furthermore his totally secular and somewhat cynical version takes away from pastoral the authority of Christian insights about the inversions of hierarchy, the casting down of the mighty from their thrones, and the exalting of the lowly.

Rural Sports had foundered on the question of labor. Against what he presents as the fruitless labors of the town, Gay has only rural leisure activities to oppose, since the actual work of the countryside is a lower-class occupation and he has no full aristocratic sense of the role of the great estate. He tries to blur the distinction between work and play in the country by calling the "happy fields" the "kind rewarders of industrious life" (431). His earlier rural poem in fact testifies to its own marginality.

In *The Shepherd's Week* Gay is continuing the aristocratic prejudices of neoclassic pastoral in parodying attempts at realism and in showing the work of his shepherds to be sweaty and vulgar. Yet he also necessarily presents their work as central, and indeed to a considerable degree as healthy and robust:

'Twas in the Season when the Reaper's Toil
Of the ripe Harvest 'gan to rid the Soil;
Wide through the Field was seen a goodly Rout,
Clean Damsels bound the gather'd Sheaves about,
The Lads with sharpen'd Hook and sweating Brow
Cut down the Labours of the Winter Plow.

("Saturday," 7–12, vol. 1, p. 119)

As John Barrell says, Gay as a poet may have needed to believe in the aristocratic preconceptions, but as a member of a good but decayed family he was in no position to endorse them without reservation. The decline in the traditions of aristocratic leisure has itself contributed to the decline of pastoral. The middling gentry's suspicion of aristocratic idleness combines here with the new interest in labor brought about by the growth in agrarian capitalism. An older, quasi-feudal, Squire-Western sense of closeness to these realities fights against the polite disdain. But the problem about polite labor remains. Gay is in a sense evading it by writing a poem with only an oblique relevance to the matter.

A part of the sense of privilege that he confirms in his polite readers is the recognition that they do not have to work with their hands, although they are at the same time reassured that the rural poor are happy and they are indeed encouraged into the luxury of envying them to some degree.[20]

Trivia is less oblique in its examination of modern politeness, although evasive enough for all that. It reveals Gay's difficulty in placing himself between the two major ideological traditions. For the poem cannot be read as a condemnation of the corrupt upstarts of the town from the landed gentry's traditional perspective of stable rural order. The implication behind the mock-heroic of Trivia is not that there has been a terrible degeneration from the ethos of its classical prototype. Gay's mock-heroic tone incorporates a certain sense of diminishment, but it also conveys genuine enjoyment. Trivia, although it certainly does not ignore the dirt and danger of London, is also full of the attractive liveliness and variety of its sights and sounds. The town ladies who, "gayly dress'd, the Mall adorn / With various Dyes, and paint the sunny Morn," are like pretty fawns and birds, for "The Seasons operate on every Breast" (1. 145–6, 151). Gay here gently punctures the town's pretensions to an art and a politeness above nature. Yet the corollary of this is that town life is allowed to share in the brightness of spring. It is not in the last analysis traumatically alienated from nature.

On the other hand, Gay is always equally aware that the polite world is not usually innocent, spontaneous, and natural. The sallow milkmaid of the town is sadly unlike the "Milk-maid of the Plains" (2. 12). He does not try to suffuse the details of London life with the religious significance Virgil gave agriculture. His city poem is secular and demystified. Although the poem is influenced by Addison's and Steele's prose city georgics written in celebration of the hive of industry that is London, Gay does not engage in quasi-religious eulogies of commerce either. But this leaves him with a problem in finding an equivalent for agriculture in Virgil. He praises and celebrates lower-class urban work, but he certainly cannot make it central in a polite poem. He prettifies it by mythology on occasions, but he also presents polite, almost obsessive injunctions about how to avoid the dirt and inconvenience it causes passersby.[21]

It is walking that he presents as his central georgic activity. This idea is itself a mock-heroic joke, of course, and a device for getting us through London. But it is also a way of evading a genuine problem about polite labor. True georgic had always been able to turn its central activity into a symbolic art of living as well as a form of labor. Gay associates his walking with an unspecified "Business" and also with the idea of exercise. The poet contrasts himself explicitly with those who loll in coaches and sedan chairs, the decadent upper classes, the *nouveaux riches*, and those who walk idly like fops. Yet his own walking is obviously a leisure activity too. The walker has time to remark on all he sees, to stop and browse at book-stalls, and to taste oysters. "Walking" thus has a very precise and revealing class orientation in the poem. It carries moralistic gentry condemnation of a decadent aristocratic idleness, but in its evasive half-work half-leisure status it is a kind of golden mean between idleness and the vulgar labors of the lower classes. But, of course, "walking" cannot provide a solution to the polite conflict of leisure and labor in the period. In presenting it as both work and leisure, Gay evades the necessity of making it either. It is not meant to be taken seriously as an equivalent to agriculture in Virgil, and it is because Gay cannot find a convincing alternative for his time that he needs the saving grace of mock heroic.

Where walking can attain certain symbolic, art-of-living dimensions is in its close relationship to the theme of manners. Richard Sennet points out that walking in the streets acquired an importance as a social activity in the eighteenth century that it had never had before.[22] The ability to respond appropriately to those you met, most of whom in a large city were inevitably strangers, was a most important decorum for the time and one that could not depend on the old fixities.

Gay's walker therefore gives instructions in the normative patterns of behavior, and the poem reaches an uncharacteristically sustained earnestness of tone on the subject.

> Let due Civilities be strictly paid.
> The Wall surrender to the hooded Maid;
> Nor let thy sturdy Elbow's hasty Rage
> Justle the feeble Steps of trembling Age:
> And when the Porter bends beneath his Load,
> And pants for Breath; clear thou the crouded Road.
> But, above all, the groping Blind direct,
> And from the pressing Throng the Lame protect.
> You'll sometimes meet a Fop, of nicest Tread,
> Whose mantling Peruke veils his empty Head,
> At ev'ry Step he dreads the Wall to lose,
> And risks, to save a Coach, his red-heel'd Shoes,
> Him, like the *Miller* pass with Caution by,

Lest from his Shoulder Clouds of Powder fly.
But when the Bully, with assuming Pace,
Cocks his broad Hat, edg'd round with tarnish'd Lace,
Yield not the Way; defy his strutting Pride,
And thrust him to the muddy Kennels side;
He never turns again, nor dares oppose;
But mutters coward Curses as he goes.

(2. 45–64)

These couplets make up a reliable set of instructions, even if the
reader senses a certain fussiness. The passage is full of the details
of town life and yet is generalising in its force, with personifica-
tions like "trembling Age" and generic phrases like "the groping
Blind." The satire on dress gains weight from the fact that in
these conditions the clothes in a sense *are* the man. The bully's
lace is, of course, metaphorically as well as literally "tarnish'd,"
and the fop's foolishly elaborate wig is the appropriate adorn-
ment for his "empty head." Gay does succeed here in differen-
tiating a true politeness from a false and in generalising the
details of etiquette into a moral campaign. It is made clear to us
that the question of taking or ceding the wall is a most important
matter of protocol and precedence in the confusions of eighteenth-century London, but also that these "due Civilities" must
be strictly paid because they are a matter of morality, of charity,
and of courage as well.

Politeness as the art of modern living in town has its own
importance. Fleetingly at least, the georgic analogy, like the heroic in Clarissa's speech in *The Rape of the Lock*, comes to
assume its own dignity, besides being mock-heroic. Ancient
values can, to some extent at least, find equivalents in the modern world. Yet Gay is speaking here after all of passing encoun-
ters that cannot fully be presented as the mores of an entire
lifestyle. If manners in town are a serious matter and genuinely
relate to moral issues, Gay deliberately juxtaposes such discussions with advice, for example, about where best to urinate in the
streets. Walking through London, in its relative inconsequen-
tiality and social fragmentation, *is* modern life for Gay, and
politeness the only way of negotiating it. Yet modern politeness
partakes of the same demystification as the world with which it
negotiates.

For politeness is a matter neither of the full aristocratic traditions of leisure nor of the real world of labor. It is also de-
politicized. There are matters, as Stephen Copley says, that are
shown to be no concern of polite verse. The sense of comedy and

diminishment is not only a factor in the quality of modern urban life but also in the poet's deliberate marginalizing of his own poem.[23]

Under the influence of Swift and Pope, Gay grew steadily more disaffected with the regime of Walpole and the corruptions of the modern ethos. In *The Beggar's Opera* he produced a truly central critique of modern mores using the criteria of an older aristocratic ideology in alliance with a popular culture that parodies the official culture only without its hypocrisy.[24]

The fact that Gay's most successful work is a play is obviously significant. The mode of drama liberates Gay, at least when he is writing, as here, from a more assured moral perspective. In poetry he has an inhibiting sense of the elevation and responsibility required to write properly on mores. The evasion of the responsibility produces deliberate brevity and a degree of marginalization. In *The Beggar's Opera* he is allowed a wider range, yet without the need for the full commitment of writing in his own person in an elevated mode. He is able to combine in characteristic fashion wit and moralism, polite sentiment and cynicism. Even here, however, the inversions have the old-fashioned pastoral effect of lending the charm of the lower-class characters to those they parody, so that moral indignation is blunted to some degree.

The second volume of the *Fables* (1737) is also written in disgust at the corruption in Walpole's England. Despite the use of the fable form, Gay writes with considerable directness. But the moral indignation of these poems often has a contrived and derivative note:

> I've heard of times, (pray God defend us,
> We're not so good but he can mend us)
> When wicked ministers have trod
> On kings and people, law and God.
> . . . .
> If schemes of lucre haunt his brain
> Projectors swell his greedy train;
> Vile brokers ply his private ear
> With jobs of plunder for the year.[25]

Gay still lacks the full ideological authority to write direct verse satire of the highest conviction. The great richness and interest of his more characteristic work lies rather in the way it both reflects and evades the conflicts of his time.

"A Kind of Artificial Good Sense": Swift and the Forms of Politeness

The "Little Decorum and Politeness We Have"

Swift wrote several tracts on the topic of politeness and was obviously proud of what he regarded as his own unusual reputation for the quality in a clergyman:

> He mov'd and bow'd and talk't with too much Grace,
> Nor shew'd the Parson in his Gait or Face.[1]

It was, indeed, he suggested, the main reason he had not received greater preferment, for in that profession,

> nothing is so fatal as the Character of Wit, Politeness in Reading, or Manners, or that Kind of Behaviour, which we contract by having too much conversed with Persons of high Station and Eminency; these Qualifications being reckoned by the *Vulgar* of *all Ranks* to be Marks of *Levity*.[2]

Yet Swift is also notorious as the author of some of the least polite poems in the language. He speaks disparagingly of all his poetry, which shows in a marked way the tendency to use verse as a *less* serious way of writing than prose. These poems are now at last, however, the recipients of considerable critical attention. And rightly so, of course, for Swift's peculiar version of the occasional poet's mode is not really, like that of his friends', a withdrawal from seriousness so much as a deeply paradoxical way of showing the seriousness of his own concern for poetry and mores.

Swift's earliest poems, the odes, are highly revealing attempts at the laureate mode in praise of William III, Archbishop Sancroft, and others. They aspire to the "Spirit of Exalted Poetry" ("Ode to the King," 46), but their tone is constantly interrupted by a low realism, a satiric sense that Swift finds difficult to combine with his hoped-for elevations:

> Our Prince has hit Him, like *Achilles*, in the *Heel*,
> The poys'nous Darts has made him reel,
> Giddy he grows, and down is hurl'd,
> And as a Mortal to his *Vile Disease*,
> Falls sick in the *Posteriors* of the World.
>
> ("Ode to the King," 142–46, p. 7)

Swift's later bitter attacks on poets and court patronage are well-known, but the indignation of "Directions for a Birth-day Song" or "On Poetry: a Rapsody" is fired partly by his remembrance of the ideal tradition. In "On Reading Dr. Young's Satires" he gives, in a sarcastic context, the clearest summary of the mores ideal:

> For, such is good Example's Pow'r,
> It does its Office ev'ry Hour,
> Where *Governors* are good and wise;
> Or else the truest Maxim lyes.
>
> (19–22, p. 307)

The "Ode to the Athenian Society" sets forth a modernized version of the same program in unironic fashion, for Philosophy has been appointed by heaven

> To be the great Original
> For Man to *dress* and *polish* his Uncourtly Mind.
>
> (217–18, p. 15)

The Athenian Society periodical writers have thus done great service in making philosophy polite and spreading such knowledge.

But if politeness is of great importance to Swift, he increasingly, of course, finds it in very short supply, under great threat, and constantly mimicked by false forms. In "our Northern Climate" in particular, he writes, "all the little Decorum and Politeness we have are purely forced by Art, and are so ready to lapse into Barbarity."[3]

Ideologically, he is very much involved in the defense of the landed interest against what he and others saw as the growing luxury and decadence of a commercial society. He is much less willing than Pope to compromise with these developments and to attempt to mold them in conservative directions. He does not believe it can or should be done. His stance is oppositional almost from the first. His political, social, and religious preconceptions necessitated opposition to the financiers, to Protestant dissent, and to what might be considered the more bourgeois forms of politeness. In "A Pastoral Dialogue Between Richmond-Lodge and Marble-Hill," Marble-Hill house is made to say,

> Some *South Sea* Broker from the City,
> Will purchase me, the more's the Pity,
> Lay all my fine Plantations waste,
> To fit them to his Vulgar Taste.
>
> (67–70, p. 324)

An idiosyncratic combination of gentry moralism and Restoration exhibitionism and scepticism gives Swift powerful ideological weapons against the new ethos. It was far easier to condemn what was new, however, than to find a positive alternative perspective. Although Swift condemns the slide from mores into politeness more passionately than anyone else in the period, he has in fact no very clear system of traditional mores in mind himself to oppose to the new developments. For him the "highest Period of Politeness in *England* [was] the peaceable Part of King *Charles* the First's Reign".[4] Politeness here is obviously an umbrella word for cultural health. But Swift's is a remarkably demystified view of hierarchy and authority. He is, as C. J. Rawson has said, an anti-Hobbesian with a Hobbesian view of human nature and a Hobbesian conception of some of the functions of government.[5] Authority and order are of the utmost importance, but there is no sense of mystery or ancient sanctions about them, as there certainly is at times in Pope. This is true even in Swift's religious thought. In *Sentiments of a Church of England Man*, for example, he writes that he is not certain that episcopal government is of divine origin, but that it is necessary for order. He has a strong Augustinian sense of human depravity, and he uses his own orthodox criteria to attack the Whig Socinianism and freethinking of the new age, but he is hardly noted for his rich presentation of the positive truths of Christian salvation.

Swift's views on the aristocratic ideal and on the importance of birth have the same tone. His politics and his propaganda against the Whigs necessitated presenting them as plebians attempting to usurp an ordained patrician order. In *The Examiner* No. 40 (10 May 1711), "a Contempt for *Birth, Family* and *ancient Nobility*" is one of the "Heresies in Politicks" propagated by the Whigs.[6] Swift genuinely believes in nobility and in the ideal system of norms associated therewith. He writes, for example, that young noblemen should be educated to be "Patterns of Politeness." Yet again the system is a demystified one, part of the natural order of things certainly, but not associated with a rich generosity and graciousness. In a comment on Harley, Lord Oxford, he criticises him for overvaluing the accident of birth. Elsewhere he defends the ideal of nobility, but on somewhat naturalistic and rationalist grounds—the superior education the nobility ideally ought to have received, the example of noble ancestors, and the possession of property.[7]

Furthermore, Swift's political situation forces him into an increasingly strident attack upon the contemporary aristocracy as such for being now in alliance, in his view, with Walpole, with the financiers, and with a corrupt court. He announces that only one in thirty aristocrats, or even fewer, has received the appropriate education, and he is scathing about the decadence and superficiality of the upper classes of his time (*Prose Works* 4, 228).

In Swift's theoretical essays on politeness, revealingly enough, his criteria for evaluation are not the older aristocratic ones but a version of "civility"—the partially demystified justification of manners not as the preordained mores of a whole social group but as explicable in terms of reason and good sense. Reason is the true source of good manners (*Prose Works* 8, 213), and not the artificial ceremonies of particular societies. But if stoic universalism is the origin of this view, it has an inbuilt elitism behind its apparent democratic tendency, and this appeals to Swift. In fact he takes it further, combining it with a characteristic pessimism. If reason as the basis for true civility should be available to all, it is in practice "a gift which very few among mankind are possessed of." The rules and conventions of particular societies therefore remain necessary. "All the civilized nations of the world have agreed upon fixing some rules for common behavior, best suited to their general customs, as a kind of artificial good sense to supply the defects of reason."[8]

So Swift's thought tends to demystify convention and tradition at the same time as it puts an enormous conservative weight on time-honored institutions and laws, those "common forms" that he implicitly recommends in the *The Tale of a Tub* as the sole refuge against fanaticism. A strain of personal arrogance and singularity complicates the picture further, the half-hint that he himself is one of those "very few among mankind" who *are* possessed of reason. The implication sometimes seems to be that for such men the "rules for common behaviour" to "supply the defects of reason" are less necessary and can perhaps be ignored. Vanessa reflects back to Swift as his own maxim, "That common forms were not design'd / Directors to a noble Mind" ("Cadenus and Vanessa," 612–13). The word "noble" is interesting here. An elitism that was originally class-based is retained and even intensified by being transformed into a purely personal mode in the absence of its traditional supports.

As early as 1710 Swift had written of the Whigs that England had for the last twenty years "lain under the Influence of such Counsels and Persons, whose Principle and Interest it was to corrupt our Manners, blind our Understandings, drain our Wealth, and in Time destroy our Constitution both in Church and State."[9] His pessimism about his society steadily increased after the fall of the Tories and then Walpole's long tenure in office. He comes to feel less and less hope of reestablishing ideological control over the new developments, presenting himself instead as one whose "*Principles*, of antient date, / Ill suit with those profess'd of late" ("Life and Character of Dr. Swift," 146–47). If it was hard for Swift to find a positive way of relating mores and manners without the full support of the old ideology, it was by no means difficult for him to see the link between the corruption of mores under the Whigs and the corruption of the minutiae of polite society. In the satiric compendium *Polite Conversation*, the butts—Wagstaff and his friends—are, of course, Whigs. The word "polite" itself, as in that work, increasingly becomes a satiric one for Swift, an index of the false politeness of a decadent society. True civility has been subverted by an empty superficial politeness, a mechanical mimicry of fashionable behavior by middle-class social climbers, or a vacuous self-indulgence by the upper classes:

> We are forced to take up with the poor Amusements of Dress and Visiting, or the more pernicious ones of Play, Drink and Vicious Amours, whereby the Nobility and Gentry of both Sexes are entirely corrupted both in Body and Mind.[10]

Swift retains belief in a true civility that ideally is linked with true culture and learning as well as with true religion, but he finds less and less evidence of any of them in his own society. He writes to Archbishop King that he tries to avoid pessimism, but

I compare true Religion to Learning and Civility which have ever been in the world, but very often shifted their scenes; sometimes leaving whole Countries where they have long flourished and removing to others that were before barbarous; which hath been the case of Christianity itself, particularly in many parts of Africa, and how far the wickedness of a Nation may provoke God Almighty to inflict so great a Judgement is terrible to think.[11]

The Poet and Modern Politeness

If the great poet ideally has a responsibility for mores, the corruption of modern manners and modern poetry go together. The insipidity of "A Love Song in the Modern Taste" is not merely stylistic. It reflects the insipidity of modern attitudes to love just as surely as the flattery of modern birthday songs reflects the evils of the modern court. Swift is a more determined ancient than anyone else in his rejection of modern poetry:

So Modern Rhymers strive to blast
The Poetry of Ages past,
Which having wisely overthrown,
They from it's Ruins build their own.
("Vanburg's House," 89–92, p. 57)

But this, of course, is totally bound up with his rejection of modern mores.

Swift's adoption of the amateur occasional mode has therefore a different meaning than it does in Parnell or Prior. It enacts Swift's own peculiar version of stylishness and social pride, but his assertion of his amateur status is much more violent than anyone else's:

A COPY of Verses kept in the Cabinet, and only shewn to a few Friends, is like a Virgin much sought after and admired; but when printed and published, is like a common Whore whom any body may purchase for half a Crown.[12]

This obviously includes a quasi-aristocratic *sprezzatura*, but its tone is very different, a tone finely described in another context by C. J. Rawson as an *hauteur* that has "a fervour . . . very different from the cool confident lordliness of a Chesterfield: a fervour which may derive from a commitment to aristocratic values, shot through with an anxiety of not belonging."[13] Swift clearly goes far beyond the conventional attitudes here in the degree of his disgust at the commercialization of literature, which he regards, significantly, as the marketing of self-revelation.

Yet Swift does profit from the evasion of the inhibiting demands of public decorum that the lighter forms of occasional verse permit him. Virginia Woolf writes of the *Journal to Stella,*

> In any highly civilized society disguise plays so large a part, politeness is so essential, that to throw off the ceremonies and conventions and talk a "little language" for one or two to understand, is as much a necessity as a breath of air in a hot room. The reserved, the powerful, the admired, have the most need of such a refuge. Swift himself found it so.[14]

The same conditions apply for much of Swift's poetry. The amateur occasional poet's freedom and spontaneity, the relaxation of the obligation to publish, the evasion of the decorums of the higher kinds—all encourage a sense of fun, a closeness to the racy elements of common life, and at times an emotional self-expression that might not otherwise have come easily to him.

In that strange poem "Cadenus and Vanessa" Swift cunningly exploits the conditions of intimate occasional verse and at the same time the newer forms of publication. The situation is, after all, an embarrassing one that could have subjected Swift to public ridicule or scandal. It puts the greatest possible demands on his social and literary politeness. He provides a psychological explanation for the fact that Esther has fallen in love with him, praises her enthusiastically, says how flattered and attracted he is, and at the same time tries tactfully to put her off. The poem was obviously written first and foremost to her. Yet the convention of a purely personal manuscript poem was less real by this time, and "Cadenus and Vanessa," in its length, formality, and mythological elaboration, certainly does not have that feel to it. The poem has to exist in a public dimension to an extent because Swift's whole purpose is precisely to distance the private emotions and conflict by creating something separate from them, an artifact. He sets his poem in the interface between the private and public worlds and between genuinely occasional manuscript poems and the conventional pose of being such. For Swift is able at the end to withdraw the public dimension he has conferred. He reverts to the saving grace of privacy, refusing that "world" to which he has to some extent appealed the privilege of knowledge:

> But what Success *Vanessa* met,
> Is to the World a Secret yet:
>
> . . . .
>
> Must never to Mankind be told,
> Nor shall the conscious Muse unfold.
>
> (818–19; 826–27)

Swift's tactful strategy also includes setting Vanessa up as a contrast to the whole modern polite attitude to relations between the sexes. As much of his work makes clear, this was not just a strategem for a particular poem. He genuinely believes that the area of sexual relationships is one of the most obvious indexes of the decadence of modern politeness and modern polite poetry. Ideally, women are a great civilizing agent, and the refusal to admit them properly to social life has led to a decline in modern politeness. Yet at the same Swift also undeniably projects on to women as the "low-Other" all the dirt and carnality that true civilization needs to cover up and control.[15]

Occasional and semi-private poems are an appropriate mode in which to deal with the issue of relationships with women, and Swift's work in this area obviously has ideological and exemplary purposes. As critics have for some time recognized, he is trying to revise love poetry in favor of a demystified relationship based on virtue and friendship:

> With Friendship and Esteem possest,
> I n'er admitted Love a Guest.

If his satires on women are unusually violent for the period, he is also less inclined to write patronizingly, as Ellen Pollak has shown,[16] in his recommendation of reason and virtue.

Yet it is the desire to correct contemporary illusions that comes across with the greatest force. Swift sees love sentiment in both a moralistic and a commonsensical way, rejecting it as a false idealization, a delusion, a stimulus to or a covering for immorality. As with manners, he has no older aristocratic values to oppose to new developments, since he rejects the old courtly modes just as firmly as the new sentimentalism. His attitudes seem to come from the moral rigorism of the middling Anglican gentry, suspicious both of the court and of the excesses of bourgeois sentimentalism. They can be paralleled in Jeremy Collier, John Dennis, and even Samuel Richardson; but not the violent language and sarcastic wit of the rejection:

> Or should a Porter make Enquiries
> For *Chloe, Sylvia, Phillis, Iris;*
> Be told the Lodging, Lane, and Sign,
> The Bow'rs that those Nymphs divine;
> Fair *Chloe* would perhaps be found
> With Footmen tippling under Ground,
> The charming *Silvia* beating Flax,
> Her Shoulders mark'd with bloody Tracks;
> Bright *Phillis* mending ragged Smocks,
> And radiant *Iris* in the Pox.
>> ("To Stella who Collected and Transcribed his Poems,"
>> 39–48, p. 185)

Swift's so-called scatological poems are now quite correctly perceived to be the products of the same intense moral indignation.[17] Polite sentiment in its foolish ignoring of physicality unrealistically idealizes women, and it is Swift's role to disabuse. In "Strephon and Chloe," for example, Chloe begins as "so genteel and nice," the idealized love object of a polite love poetry that is *précieux* in style and of the *beau monde:*

> What ogling, sighing, toasting, vowing!
> What powder'd Wigs! What Flames and Darts!
> What Hampers full of bleeding Hearts!
> What Sword-knots! What poetic Strains!
> What Billet-doux and Clouded Cains!
>> (34–39, p. 520)

As so often in Swift's work, the moral rigorism of the Anglican gentry combines curiously here with Restoration court cynicism, while the disgusting physical explicitness has itself evolved from the antifeminist and libertine traditions of the court wits, especially Rochester. Swift has to engage with physicality and vulgarity himself to show the hollowness of the illusion that makes up Strephon's polite sentiment.

But when the wedding night disabuses Strephon he reacts not with disgust but with a vulgar acceptance that, as Rawson shows, can hardly have Swift's support either. For it is surely Swift's own horror at the omnipresence of dirt and carnality that makes him so aware of the folly of pretending it does not exist. The constant emphasis on cleanliness is obviously a personal concern of Swift's, but it also relates to the growing "polite" feeling of separation from the juices and odors of others' bodies that Norbert Elias describes as a crucial factor in the growth and spread of politeness and the "civilising process."[18] Swift dislikes the way the couple accommodates their own physicality almost as much as he dislikes the illusion that it does not exist. What he recommends instead is certainly not a genial recognition of the flesh, but an awareness of the impossibility of pretending it away. This is his quarrel with eighteenth-century politeness—not its attempt to minimize unpleasantness but its complacency in thinking it has succeeded. Instead we need constant vigilance. The social fiction he recommends is in a sense a mean between the old idealizations and open vulgarity, because one party at least is aware of the fiction and of what needs to be covered up:

> But, after Marriage, practise more
> Decorum that she did before,
> To keep her Spouse deluded still,
> And make him fancy what she will.
>
> (141–44)

We remain aware of paradoxes and potential contradictions here and of Swift's own uncertainties about convention and fiction. These lines remind us, after all, of happiness as a "perpetual possession of being well deceived." Swift himself often works to unmask what polite surfaces cover. In "Dick, a Maggot" Dick uses a fashionable powder to mask his "gypsey Visage" in polite society, but Swift points out that this only makes it stand out the more clearly, "like a fresh Turd just dropt on Snow." But Swift is attempting to make a distinction between false politeness and true. Flaying the woman and gutting the beau should not be necessary, and it should not surprise us that what they reveal is unpleasant. The surprise is an index of the complacency of eighteenth-century politeness and of its failure to register the true horror of what threatens civilization. This is a superficial covering up of unpleasantness, a gloss over it, and a complacent pretence that it does not exist. It is only as a weapon against this complacency that Swift operates by, in a sense, flaying the woman himself in these poems. As C. J. Rawson says, although "we must in some sense face the reality of the flayed woman and the gutted beau . . . decency and civilisation demand that they also be kept out of sight."[19] True politeness accepts the existence of unpleasantness, and there is no need therefore to pry beneath the surface, for there is no complacency or self-deluding fiction to destroy.

But the distinctions Swift is trying to make between true and false politeness, successful and reprehensible coverings, deluding and nondeluding fictions remain problematic ones. He affirms a proper "decency" and "decorum," but they are themselves demystified. They are barriers against chaos and anarchy rather than sources of rich and traditional fulfillment. They are presented as very necessary but, at least in modern circumstances, very minimalist and precarious achievements indeed. And whatever Swift intends, he seems himself at times to express an element of subversive delight in their defeat, a horrified fascination with the destruction of *all* inhibitions and taboos and authorities, even those he presents as the right ones. This delight in their destruction coexists with and is indeed intensified by the powerful insistence on how necessary they are. The mysteries of Swift's psyche work together in this with his cultural disaffection as a spokesman for a resentful interest group cut off from the fullness of the old ideology.

Swift's sense of all that politeness has to define itself against is much stronger than his own recommendations of politeness. This is in part, but only in part, the paradox of the satirist whose defense of true decency in a corrupt age necessitates passionate rage and the unmasking of false politeness. He is obviously too suspicious of many aspects of contemporary politeness to be happy with the polite verse of the time. His invective, his cursing, his imagery from necromancy and the demonic are in deliberate opposition to politeness. He sounds closer at times to the learned invective of Butler and the satiric harshness of Oldham than to the politer world of early eighteenth-century verse. His work is more often satiric rejection than polite withdrawal. The tone of *vers de société* turns into savage parody, as in "Verses wrote on a Lady's Ivory Table-Book." Like Harold Pinter, Swift delights in revealing "the weasel beneath the cocktail-cabinet."

Swift is also too serious about poetry as well as too bound up with politics to opt out of public verse altogether. In one sense he bitterly refuses to accept the marginalization of poetry, although in another sense he is forced into marginalization himself by modern circumstances. His allegiances, like Pope's, lie ultimately in the tradition of the poet as commentator on mores. He affirms that only "heavenly influence" can inspire true poetry, and he praises such poetry warmly:

Unjustly poets we asperse;
Truth shines the brighter clad in verse,
And all the fictions they pursue
Do but insinuate what's true.[20]

But it is the lies of false poetry of which we are made much more aware. The dangers of delusion and abuse are enormous, and high poetic flights are often a symptom of the presumption of fallen man. In particular, the false sublime is linked with the pride of the moderns, the enthusiasm of dissent, the hated "official" poetry of a corrupt politics. In "On Poetry, a Rapsody" it is a Whig poet who "for Epick claims the Bays" (129). The Renaissance laureate tradition is now inoperative, for this is a time in which "the vilest Verse thrives best at Court" (186). The only way in which true seriousness about poetry can now be expressed is by righteous indignation at its terrible abuse:

O, what Indignity and Shame,
To prostitute the Muses' Name
By flatt'ring Kings whom Heaven design'd
The Plagues and Scourges of Mankind.
                    ("On Poetry: A Rapsody," 405–8, p. 580)

It has to become almost Swift's primary aim therefore to differentiate his work from the lies of contemporary poets, the veneer of false fictions, the solemnity of "official" poetry. When he says that his verse has "No Thought, No Fancy, No Sublime" ("To Mr. Delaney," 11), he is expressing more than aristocratic self-depreciation. He overemphasizes the singsong mechanics of verse and often writes in a rough colloquial diction. *Sprezzatura* is replaced by an extreme, slapdash-sounding detachment. The popular elements Swift incorporates into his attack on a falsely polite society are not the warm and earthy ones of Gay's quasi-feudal approach but a Restoration demotic imbued with an aristocratic wit's contempt for the mob and then inverted against the upper classes themselves. Instead of opting out of the realm of public verse altogether, Swift writes political squibs, ballads and lampoons, occasional verse of the most ephemeral type, expressing in his lowly kinds and in his very style an absolute contempt for what he describes.:

LET them, when they once get in
Sell the Nation for a Pin;
While they sit a picking Straws

Let them rave of making Laws;
While they never hold their Tongue,
Let them dabble in their Dung;
Let them form a grand Committee,
How to plague and starve the City;
Let them stare and storm and frown
When they see a Clergy-Gown.
Let them, 'ere they crack a Louse,
Call for th'Orders of the House;
Let them with their gosling Quills,
Scribble senseless Heads of Bills;
We may, while they strain their Throats,
Wipe our Arses with their Votes.

("The Legion Club," 47–62, pp. 602–3)

This is, of course, the deliberate inversion of high seriousness, not the polite evasion of it. Indeed, as J. A. Downie shows, "On Poetry, a Rapsody" links the degeneration of poetry with the degeneration of political order in a way that reveals it to be in a sense a poem still in the tradition of commentary on mores, although only, as it were, by negation, a negation that includes style.[21] Swift has the ideological confidence to reject modern politeness with the greatest conviction. Contemporary mores have so far degenerated that to comment on them properly at all requires a tone conveying contempt and repudiation. But the positive ideological norms he espouses have never really amounted to a powerful alternative to what has gone wrong. He does not have enough imaginative faith in the past or hope for the future to be able to make positive claims to laureate verse himself.

For his inversion of the mores tradition reflects not only contempt for modern manners, but also a real despair about society's ever being otherwise. In "Verses on the Death of Dr. Swift" he affirms the possibility of true heroism, true public spirit, and even true political action in the teeth of a corrupt society:

Fair LIBERTY was all his Cry;
For her he stood prepar'd to die;
For her he boldly stood alone;
For her he oft expos'd his own.

. . . .

HAD he but spar'd his Tongue and Pen,
He might have rose like other Men:
But Power was never in his Thought;
And, Wealth he valu'd not a Groat.

This has become the most discussed of all Swift's poems and I have no wish to add to the volume of general commentary.[22] What is clear, however, is that the false politeness of the new order is condemned not by the social standards and mores of an old order, but rather in contrast to what is presented as a purely personal achievement.

8

"To Form the Manners": Pope and the Poetry of Mores

Mores and the Laureate Poet

To regard Pope as a polite poet in the sense of being simply a spokesman for a polite society would be as limiting and as misleading as to regard him as the poet of an "Age of Reason." But the young Pope is extremely interested in the externals of polite and fashionable behavior and almost pathetically eager to establish his credentials as a man about town. As he grows older, he takes extraordinary care to present himself as a gentleman in his villa, whom "even *Envy* must own" lives "among the Great." Politeness is relevant not only to his self-presentation but also to his conception of the role of the poet. It is central in fact to his ideological purposes as a whole. It lies at the heart of his great enterprise of assimilating his contemporary world to the standards of the past.[1]

Identifying with the landed interest and the gentry, Pope regarded the aristocracy as the leaders of his class. He believed erroneously but with apparent sincerity that his own family was a branch of an aristocratic one. In the "Epistle to Dr. Arbuthnot" he supplied the following note: "Mr. *Pope's* Father was of a Gentleman's family in *Oxfordshire*, the Head of which was the Earl of *Downe*" (note to line 381). He was convinced that:

> Of gentle Blood (part shed in Honour's Cause
> While yet in *Britain* Honour had Applause)
> Each Parent sprung.
>
> (388–90, p. 611)

His formative relations with the Catholic higher gentry worked in the same direction.

Ideologically, therefore, Pope looks back to a system in which good manners as well as aesthetic taste are regarded as the index of an ordained social fitness to rule. His early work in particular links good manners normatively with the court and aristocracy, and he praises Roscommon for his "Manners gen'rous as his Noble Blood" (*Essay on Criticism* 726, p. 168). In conversation with Spence he agrees that there is such a thing as "the nobleman look," although he expounds this as "that look which noblemen should have, rather than what they have generally now."[2] His imaginative response to the old proaristocratic ideology is a genuinely powerful one. In the "Epistle to Burlington," for example, he reveals a stronger sense of the Renaissance ideas of the great estate as a microcosm and of the positive dimensions of aristocratic leisure than any other poet of the time.

Pope's attitudes, nevertheless, inevitably reflect the decline of the old ideology as well. The fact that, whatever his illusions, his own background might really be regarded as middle-rank contributes to that special *hauteur* shown by non-aristocratic poets with aristocratic allegiances, but it also entails a degree of demystification. The aristocratic wit to which Pope is attracted is mediated through the scepticism of the Restoration court. This combines oddly with an old-fashioned gentry-style moralism, which, dependent on aristocratic ideology in some ways, is deeply disapproving in others. Yet Pope clearly also regards himself as in many ways a modern, enlightened figure ("For Modes of Faith, let graceless zealots fight" (*Essay on Man* 3. 305). He gives a highly demystified account of the origins of monarchy in the *Essay on Man* and also there attacks the idea that aristocratic blood as such has any merit. The breakup of the old ideology gave the expression of this traditional sentiment that "Worth makes the man" (4. 203) a more progressive emphasis. Pope's frequent stress on sincerity and the "honest muse" is obviously a reaction to the partial loss of belief in the innate link between aristocracy and virtue, although his continued association of honor with the aristocracy shows a split in his mind. In the "Epistle to Bathurst," for example, he addresses the few good aristocrats and hopes that with them "Honour" may "linger ere it leaves the land" (248, p. 581).

Pope's discussions of politeness thus consist of an attempt to mediate between gentry and aristocratic attitudes and between old and new. He comments, for example, that the "prevailing notion of genteelness consisting in freedom and ease has led many to a total neglect of decency." He attempts himself, like so many writers of the time, to distinguish true politeness from false:

True politeness consists in being easy oneself and making everybody
about one as easy as we can. But the mistaking brutality for freedom
(for which so many of our young people of quality have made themselves so remarkable of late) has just the contrary effect.[3]

But the balancing act is fine one. Politeness obviously continues
to consort with "freedom and ease" in a quasi-aristocratic manner rather than with respectable "decency" alone, but it must be
reconciled with such decency. The problematic of politeness
reveals Pope's modification of old values and his simultaneous
attempt to assimilate new values to traditional models.

The new capitalism and commercialism were the most obvious
influences necessitating revisions of the old ethos. From Pope's
perspective the new developments were threatening.

For money upon money increases, copulates and multiplies, and
guineas beget guineas in *saecula saeculorum*.

In particular he attacks the consequent social upheaval:

And Hemsley, once proud Buckingham's delight,
Slides to a Scriv'ner or a City Knight.[4]

A revealing phrase from the "Epistle to Cobham" makes one
example of human instability the way that manners shift "with
Fortunes" (1. 166).

Yet if Pope is less inclined than Swift to demystify the great
sanctions of the past, he is also much less likely to reject contemporary society out of hand. His interests cut across party lines, as
in his friendship with Lord Burlington. The landed interest as a
whole, not to mention the upper aristocracy as such, was implicated in the new capitalism by investment and borrowing for
agrarian improvement. Pope disapproves of many aspects of this,
but he also believes that some of the benefits of the new developments can be grasped while their effects are contained within
traditional constraints. Pope refuses to allow either the contemporary aristocracy or the new consumerism to escape moral
scrutiny, but the other side of this is that he believes that politeness can be channelled into suitably modified patterns of
mores. The task can and must be done. Order and morality can
still be imposed.

Unlike Swift, Pope thus aims, for the major part of his career, at
a certain centrality and comprehensiveness. The bias is con-

servative, but not to such an extent that he is put at odds with the consensus, for:

> In *Words*, as *Fashions*, the same Rule will hold,
> Alike Fantastick, if *too New* or *Old*;
> Be not the *first* by whom the *New* are try'd,
> Nor yet the *last* to lay the *Old* aside.
>
> (*Essay on Criticism*, 333–36, p. 154)

In *Windsor Forest* Pope makes clear his ambition to combine rural order and Stuart hierarchy with the benefits of the new commerce. The poem has a richer sense of the aristocratic traditions of leisure than others in the period, and Pope succeeds, despite his personal dislike for the pastime, in giving hunting a more genuine significance than did Gay in *Rural Sports*. His sense of the philosophical significance of retirement is similarly far richer than Parnell's in "Health." He is able to combine this emphasis, however, with the new interest in labor and commerce, although, as a recent critic has pointed out, there is a remnant of the older aristocratic attitude in Pope's refusal to look closely at the details of either.[5]

Windsor Forest, in the centrality of its ambitions, is clearly a poem in the laureate tradition, although Pope modestly transfers this status to the poem Granville will write and purports to be no more than a pastoral poet himself. But from very early in his career, Pope's ideological interests combine with his personal ambition to lead him toward the great humanist model of the poet as guide to and spokesman for the ruling class and as custodian of mores in the line of Virgil and Horace, Spenser, Ben Jonson, and Dryden. He comments on Homer that "In ancient times Princes entertain'd in their families certain learned and wise men, who were both Poets and Philosophers, and not only made it their business to amuse and delight, but to promote wisdom and morality." He also quotes Bossu's remark that epic poems are created to "form the Manners." In another significant early statement he makes clear his belief that the court is the proper source of patronage, for:

> when Shakespeare's performances had merited the protection of his prince, and when the encouragement of the court had succeeded to that of the town, the works of his riper years are manifestly raised above those of the former.[6]

Even after the death of Queen Anne, he continues this tradition in more difficult circumstances, influencing the tastes of the aristocracy through personal contact as well as by his poetry, in for example, the matter of landscape gardening.[7] His concern with the manners and mores of other classes continues and modifies the great poet's traditional role of commenting on and guiding the whole nation's behavior. Despite the demystification in which he himself participates, he is able to project enough imaginative faith in the old ideology to give him an authority as a poet that his friends cannot sustain, and he is open enough to the new developments to avoid the marginalization from which much of their work suffers. He refers frequently to the laureate role in its true sense, as opposed to the court office held by such as Cibber, and claims it unequivocally for himself, although in so doing his position becomes more and more paradoxical, as will be seen.

Pope's genuine commitment to the fullness of this Renaissance role obviously marks him as a more dedicated poet than any other of his time. He "lisp'd in Numbers, for the Numbers came," and his writing, the "unweary'd Mill" of his verses, was always his full-time occupation. His sense of vocation is elevated, and the imagery of his Catholicism surrounds his rendingly serious dedication to his art:

> To write well, lastingly well, Immortally well, must not one leave Father and Mother and cleave unto the Muse? Must not one be prepared to endure the reproaches of Men, want and much Fasting, nay Martyrdom in its Cause?[8]

Necessarily, therefore, Pope distinguishes his work from that of the courtly amateurs and occasional poets, the "Mob of Gentlemen who wrote with Ease" ("Imitations of Horace, Ep. 2. 1," 108). It is not the task, he writes, "of an Heroic Poet like myself to sing at marriages, burials, Christenings etc."[9] He appeals to the full tradition of Renaissance humanist poetry, avoiding what had become the superficiality of the amateur mode. He remarks that Richard Crashaw:

> writ like a gentleman, that is at leisure hours, and more to keep out of idleness than to establish a reputation. . . . No man can be a true poet who writes for diversion only

Elsewhere he writes:

Lord Dorset's things are all excellent in their way; for one should consider his pieces as a sort of epigram: wit was his talent—He and Lord Rochester should be considered as holiday writers; as gentlemen that diverted themselves now and then with poetry, rather than as poets.

From such poets it would be unjust to expect anything "that regards design, form, fable (which is the soul of poetry), nor anything that concerns exactness, or consent of the parts (which is the body)."[10]

Yet the occasional-amateur tradition has a considerable influence on Pope, despite its being incompatible with his deepest aspirations. He borrows from its gracefulness and stylish wit and lays claim to its social and literary prestige at various times. In the preface to his 1717 Works, in particular, he adopts the traditional pose of the gentlemanly occasional poet. Poetry and criticism are "only the affair of idle men who write in their closets and of idle men who read there"; he "writ because it amused me; [and] published because I was told I might please such as it was a credit to please." He demands, "What critic can be so unreasonable as not to leave a man time enough for any more serious employment?"[11] In his letters, too, he often depreciates poetry in the conventional way, and his own disdain for professional writers in The Dunciad has the old social prejudice behind it, as well as literary considerations.

Widening criteria for membership in the elite had meant the spread of this originally aristocratic ideal of sprezzatura. Pope's adoption of the occasional pose shows his own aspiration to fashionable stylishness. It also obviously represents a certain social unease about his full-time commitment to poetry, despite the fact that at a more basic level the proud neoclassical status of great poet is at the heart of his whole identity. Full court patronage was not available to him after 1714. His use of the subscription method enabled him to create, in Bertrand Bronson's words, a "kind of dispersed and shared patronage."[12] He made a considerable amount of money, but the occasional-amateur's pose is obviously part of his self-distancing from bourgeois commercialization. Pope was in fact able to get the best of both worlds, reconciling the dedicated humanist tradition with an aristocratic disdain for Grub Street and yet at the same time making a living by his art. His retention of the occasional poet's stylishness is, in other words, not incompatible with a deeper responsibility for mores, as it was in the last analysis for Parnell, Prior, and Gay. As he grows increasingly disaffected politically, moreover, the occasional-amateur's pose also enables him, as will become clear, to differentiate his work from the forced decorum and artificial seriousness of the "official" poetry of the time and yet not to give up on politeness altogether.

Polite Consensus

Elements of social anxiety are evident in Pope's narrow interpretation of "polish" in the earliest phase of his career. It is a period of important training in craftsmanship, but the degree of attention to correctness suggests an excessive concern to do the right thing, even an anxiety about social acceptance.[13] In the introductory note to the pastorals he emphasizes in particular their reception by a representative sample of the polite literary elite, "Mr. Walsh, Mr. Wycherley, G. Granville afterwards Lord Lansdown, Sir William Trumbal, Dr. Garth, Lord Halifax, Lord Sommers, Mr. Mainwaring and others" (p. 123).

But Pope genuinely did achieve acceptance, influential friendships, and fame very early in his career. The growing confidence this gave him is apparent in the more relaxed tone of his verse, the more convincing sense of polite *sprezzatura* and freedom in wit:

> True Ease in Writing comes from Art, not Chance,
> As those move easiest who have learn'd to dance.[14]

An Essay on Criticism, from which these lines linking literary and social "ease" come, itself has a remarkable politeness of tone and has politeness as one of its main strands of imagery ("As Men of Breeding, sometimes Men of Wit, / T'avoid *great Errors* must be *less* commit" (259–60). Politeness is in fact central to Pope's purpose here of assimilating modern developments to all that is best from the past. He wishes to preserve what was seen in the period as the specifically aristocratic quality of wit, so that to be polite certainly includes displaying a quasi-aristocratic freedom and stylishness.[15] But to be polite must also mean being careful not to offend, and so wit has to be purified from all the Restoration excesses that the "men of sense" pointed out. It must be made appropriate to a new audience and amenable to a new consensus.

Consensus indeed is the essence of this politeness. The impolite critics of the new age, not properly instructed in the classics, need to learn good breeding, but they must be gently corrected in a tone that is itself a model of the very values it recommends. In this poem Pope comes as near as anyone would to an urbane definition of the whole creed of polite morality:

'Tis not enough your Counsel still be *true*,
Blunt Truths more Mischief than *nice Falshoods* do;
Men must be *taught* as if you taught them *not*;
And Things *unknown* propos'd as Things *forgot*:
Without *Good Breeding*, *Truth* is disapprov'd;
That only makes *Superior* Sense *Belov'd*.

(572–77)

He shows to a surprising degree a disapproval of explicit satire: "Leave dang'rous *Truths* to unsuccessful *Satyrs*" (592). He presents a civic and civil consensus, learnt from the ancients, but not slavishly imitated. His confidence that such a re-creation can be performed in his society is suggested in the very fact that impolite methods are not required.

The matter of politeness is also an essential element in and subject of Pope's earlier poems to women. Like other poets of the period, he confronts the problematic decline in the traditional conventions of love poetry, itself symptomatic of great social changes. The old aristocratic images are now redundant, but Pope never goes as far as Swift in defusing the conventions. Where he retains the old imagery he does it playfully, but in such a way that a genuine compliment is still conveyed. He preserves something of the old images as specifically social and literary fictions that convey a genuine admiration, although they also suggest the internalization of controls.

For *The Rape of the Lock* makes abundantly clear Pope's sense of the centrality of attitudes to women in his ideological purposes. The poem describes the lives of young London-based aristocrats whose leisure has degenerated into idleness. The growth of London has drawn these young people from their rural estates. An unholy alliance has developed between decadent aristocratic values and the new consumerism. The excessive language of adulation for Belinda is a combination of decadent courtly traditions and consumerist overvaluation of objects. But Belinda is also a great consumer as well as a consumer object herself. The decline of the old patriarchal controls, has allowed her far too much freedom in general.

Yet the hope of correction remains. Pope treats the spoils of commerce with which Belinda is adorned, not with unequivocal enthusiasm like Addison in the *Spectator*, but, as several critics have pointed out, not with total disapproval either.[16] It is still possible to gain the benefits of the new order without forfeiting all those of the old. If there is a sense of diminishment when this world is measured against the world of the epic past there is also the possibility of a sophisticated modern adjustment of old to new. This is still the young generation of aristocrats after all. There is still time for them to assume their responsibilities as they mature. And it is marriage that marks the first stage of that assumption of responsibility. It is important for aristocratic society that Belinda marry and that she marry the right person. As Ellen Pollak says, in Clarissa's speech echoing Sarpedon "female self-sacrifice to patriarchal marriage is evoked as both a parody and an eighteenth-century analogue to the moral heroism of a culture now defunct."[17]

Clarissa's speech represents a true politeness opposed both to a decadent aristocratic honor that is now purely a social convention and to a consumerist overvaluation of things. What it proposes, though, is good-humored consensus and correction. Pope's special politeness of tone in the poem reflects the delicacy of the task its occasion presented him. More importantly, it adjudicates between old and new, as in the *Essay on Criticism*. It shows Pope's hope that his younger generation of aristocrats can be corrected in a gentle and humorous way. It corrects the idolization of Belinda by turning it into a deliberate social compliment, and it utilizes such compliments as part of the internalization of the older patriarchal ideals, so that Belinda can be persuaded to react with good humor and marry the right man voluntarily.

No one listens to Clarissa, however. This obviously registers Pope's doubts about whether the aristocracy really will reform. The final apotheosis of the lock is a final compliment to Belinda and a final consolation suggesting that she should not take its loss too seriously. But the ending has a different sense too, and one with important concealed implications about Pope's attitudes to politeness as well as to women. His satires on women are softer than Swift's, but he has also been regarded as more patronising. Nevertheless, elements of special "degendered" sympathy have also been detected.[18] The loss of Belinda's lock could have been the prelude to the loss of her virginity in marriage, and Pope's ideological purposes still center on this. In allowing Belinda in a sense not to lose her lock at all, though, Pope is suggesting an undercurrent of feeling more clearly expressed in "Epistle to Miss Blount with the Works of Voiture,"—a feeling of identification with the freedom from convention for a young girl who does not marry.

> Marriage may all those petty Tyrants chace,
> But sets up One, a greater, in their Place;
> Well might you wish for Change, by those accurst,
> But the last Tyrant ever proves the worst.
> Still in Constraint your suff'ring Sex remains,
> Or bound in formal, or in real Chains;
> Whole Years neglected for some Months ador'd,
> The fawning Servant turns a haughty Lord;
> Ah quit not the free Innocence of Life!
> For the dull Glory of a virtuous Wife!
>
> (37–46, p. 170)

Pope himself was out of the race as far as marriage was concerned, and so there is here perhaps a relief from jealousy in the thought that young women who attract him will not marry either. But this was only one of several ways Pope was likely to take a secret pleasure in the defeat of convention, even or perhaps especially when his ideological purposes demanded its victory. Renaissance naturalist thinking underlies these lines, as in the "Elegy to the Memory of an Unfortunate Lady," so that a general questioning of convention and social ordinances is implied. The latter poem also strongly highlights the element of identification with women as *victims* of society and convention that is present as an undercurrent in *The Rape of the Lock*.

Politeness and the Correction of Manners

Pope's mature verse has always been praised for its rich urbanity. The interest in politeness is embodied in the very texture of this verse, its marvellous tact and confidence, its manipulation of tone and topical allusion. Typically Pope exploits an occasional-amateur, manuscript-poem convention, (now mainly a fiction), addressing a primary audience of particular friends and thus drawing his wider audience into a circle of which the refined social relationships of the poet himself form the center. The process is an educative one. The poems work toward a polite consensus, "Who but must laugh if such a man there be? / Who would not weep if Atticus were he?" ("Epistle to Dr. Arbuthnot," 231–14). But Pope has of course set the whole tone and the terms of the consensus from the start and thus guided the conclusion. He is therefore both inclusive and exclusive, opening up the apparently private world to the wider readership he needs, yet defining the terms of admission himself so that they seem social and moral rather than financial ones.[19] Those who will not accept the consensus and who cannot understand the ostensibly private references exclude themselves. Pope has done all he can to prevent this by the tone of polite reasonableness he usually adopts and by the deft way he makes his persona and his friends part of a recognizable context. Yet there is a quasi-aristocratic elitism here that differentiates most of Pope's work from the full public sphere and the more conduct-book attitude of Addison and Steele.

In much of this work the word "polite" is a term of praise, applied to Granville ("Epistle to Arbuthnot," 135) or to Bolingbroke (Essay on Man, 4. 382). In the Essay on Man, the Moral Essays, and various of the Horatian imitations, Pope firmly inculcates these normative patterns of moral and polite behavior. He assumes once again Spenser's role of fashioning in virtuous discipline, unsystematically but with a greater centrality and ambition than any other poet of the period. He corrects manners by example, by panegyric, and by satire, attacking false forms of politeness and its excess—Atticus, "so obliging that he n'er obliged"—as well as its deficiency.

For Pope, of course, increasingly has to engage with the realities that eighteenth-century politeness sought to control or define itself against. The first version of The Dunciad confronts a situation in which the "taste of the Rabble" is becoming the "reigning" pleasure of the "Court and Town" (note on line 2, book 1, The Dunciad Variorum, 1729). Pope's need to distance himself from the dunces must stem partly from his own sense of contamination by professionalism. In using the weapons of obscenity and physical dirt, he reveals an ambivalent fascination, like Ben Jonson, Gay, and Swift, with mud, especially urban mud. He displays a degree of enjoyment of his dunces' activities that must suggest an element of identification with their subversiveness. When all these undercurrents have been admitted, however, it can hardly, I believe, be denied that the mock-heroic in this first version of the poem is primarily and very successfully a vehicle of quasi-aristocratic disdain. By it he places his dunces perfectly, confirming C. J. Rawson's remark that his way of dealing with the threat of chaos is to keep his distance from it, defining it with the greatest precision possible.[20]

Margaret Doody has recently reminded us of the things that "made Pope the individual marginalized, critical, declassed and angry"—his position as a Catholic under the penal laws, for example.[21] These energies contribute to the power of Pope's satire, producing a degree of identification with outcasts, victims, rebels, and all those who fall foul of the official culture. But these elements appear to have a lesser place in Pope's psyche than in Swift's, or at least he masks them better. To a far greater degree than Swift, Pope contrives to give the impression that he condemns what is wrong in his society by time-honored, unquestionable sanctions. His bias remains evidently conservative, even when he condemns upper-class behavior. The proud assertion that his moral indignation overcomes any social snobbery— "And who unknown defame me, let them be / Scriblers or Peers"—is itself paradoxically expressed in the very tones of social disdain—"alike are *Mob* to me."[22]

As late as the "Epistle to Burlington" Pope is still able to present a vision of a society governed by an enlightened aristocracy. His sense of the tradition of aristocratic leisure is a far deeper one than Parnell's, Prior's, or Gay's. Instead of such leisure being evasive or marginalized, Pope presents it very clearly as the necessary foundation of and preparation for the vision of public works with which the poem concludes. As Richard Feingold has said, only those with the freedom to delight in the microcosm of their ordered estates can also have the unselfish detachment required to rule the country:

> Bid Harbors open, public Ways extend,
> Bid Temples, worthier of the God ascend;
> Bid the broad Arch the dang'rous Flood contain,
> The Mole projected break the roaring Main;
> Back to his bounds their subject Sea command,
> And roll obedient Rivers through the Land.[23]

Swift prays in "The Bubble" that God will "Quiet the raging of the Sea / And Still the Madness of the Crowd" (204). The sea in Pope's poem is similarly a symbolic one, and the building projects he recommends to the aristocracy are obviously political allegories as well as literal constructions.

But the relative certainties of the first *Dunciad* or the "Epistle to Burlington" were becoming harder to sustain. The latter itself has to evade any detailed attention to the commercial and other

processes on which the "Imperial Works" it calls for would have
to depend. The "Epistle to a Lady," written in fact like the
"Epistle to Bathurst" after the optimistic vision of "Burlington,"
shows a world in which the traditional mutability of women has
been accelerated to an alarming degree by the new leisure and
prosperity. After all the quasi-aristocratic evasions in "To Burlington," the "Epistle to Bathurst" confronts the new capitalism
directly, and the poem is impressive in its struggle to prevent the
bewildering new world from escaping from traditional moral
language and responsibilities altogether. Pope brings to his task
an imaginatively sanctioned re-creation of aristocratic ideology,
the theories of civic humanism, and Aristotelian and Christian
criteria. Yet none of them proves fully sufficient. It is difficult to
see the Man of Ross as a full counter to the society depicted in
the poem or to understand how the aristocrat Bathurst can really
teach it the "Sense to value Riches, with the Art / T'enjoy them,
and the Virtue to impart" (219–20). Nor can Pope's own theodicy
convince. As Richard Feingold says, Pope wishes always to imply that society is not a purely secular and amoral phenomenon
but part of a larger order—nature—but it is becoming more and
more problematic for him to do so.[24]

For Pope is really seeking to freeze the processes of social
change at a certain point, to go so far and then no further. His
whole endeavor is mined with contradictions. He welcomes
agrarian capitalism, for example, and some aspects of the new
commercialism while singling out the moneyed men as objects of
special distaste. Although it is perfectly possible to combine
aristocratic leadership and a conservative social order with a
developing capitalist society for a time, it is not ultimately possible to retain all the moral criteria of the old ideology in the new
circumstances.

Pope's ideological yearning for "the Integrity of ancient Nobility" has increasingly to involve a condemnation of the "modern Language of corrupted Peers."[25] His own position is, of
course, an especially paradoxical one in that he is a conservative
court poet disaffected from the contemporary court and thus
deprived of his traditional station. In the "Epistle to Dr. Arbuthnot" there dwells at the heart of the court not the true
laureate poet, but Sporus, a demonic parody of the role, a father
of lies yet an advisor to the royal family, "at the Ear of *Eve,*
familiar Toad" (319).

In such a situation it became as important to Pope as it was to
Swift to differentiate his poetry from the "official" verse of birth-

day songs and court panegyric. He had always had a strong sense of the dangers of the false sublime—a Restoration heritage—but also the true poet's hatred of the bogus. He devotes *Peri Bathous* to satire of it, and writes to the Earl of Oxford that "Our modern poets preserve a painful Equality of Fustian throughout their whole Epic or Tragic Works." In the postscript to the *Odyssey* he remarks similarly that "the *sublime* style is more easily counterfeited than the *natural*; something that passes for it or sounds like it is common to all false writers."[26] These sentiments are greatly strenghened by dislike of the poetry he parodies as describing angels surrounding George II's falling horse ("Satire 2. 1, 28).

But the nature of Pope's genius and his enormous ambition to be a great poet did not permit him to withdraw either into genteel and sociable occasional verse or into the verse merely of righteously indignant rejection. His strategy had to be a much more complex and oblique one. He comes to use the wit and *sprezzatura* of the aristocratic amateur tradition as a weapon against the false pieties of "official" verse rather than as simply an evasion of them, and he retains the capacity to comment on public mores although in paradoxical form. The tone of *sprezzatura* itself creates the impression that his poetry is not to be taken too seriously and undercuts the dangers of a pedestrian solemnity ("Some who grow dull religious strait commence / And gain in morals what they lose in sence").[27] This combines with an elegiac feeling for the instability of worldly fame and with a traditional Christian sense that art is not of any ultimate importance:

Why am I ask'd, what next shall see the light?
Heavens! was I born for nothing but to write?
Has life no Joys for me? or (to be grave)
Have I no Friend to serve, no Soul to save?
　　　　　　　　　("Epistle to Dr. Arbuthnot," 271–74, p. 606)

Yet none of this indicates lack of high seriousness or failure of nerve on Pope's part.[28] The frequent shifts of tone suit Pope's quicksilver temperament, but passages of real elevation are included within a total compound which avoids uniform solemnity in order to differentiate this work from the false sublimities of Whig panegyrical poetry and modern epic. Almost alone of the poets of his time, Pope can rise to seriousness in a way that is fully convincing, and this is precisely because he does not have to set elevated poetry apart in a realm of its own or forswear wit in order to write it.

The tone of self-depreciation in "To Mr. Fortescue" or "Epistle to Dr. Arbuthnot," for example, makes it easier to accept the growing tendency that these poems exemplify to make the poet himself an heroic figure. In apparently withdrawing like Parnell or Prior from discredited political poetry, Pope is making what is ostensibly his private life into a comment on the public realm. He gets the best of all worlds here. He is the dedicated poet and the nonchalant gentleman, the moralist who foreswears poetry and the moral poet whose life becomes art. His own lifestyle becomes a moral and political touchstone through a self-portrayal that is ironic and self-depreciating as well as exemplary.

Politeness and its Rejection

In "To Mr. Fortescue" ("Imitations of Horace, Satire 2. 1") Pope paradoxically tries to make the loss of the traditional laureate role into an advantage by claiming it anew for himself because of what he presents as the special strength of independence gained thereby. This, he says, is a court far less prepared even than the absolutist ones were to bear the truth:

> Could pension'd *Boileau* lash in honest Strain
> Flatt'rers and Bigots ev'n in *Louis'* Reign?
> Could Laureate *Dryden* Pimp and Fry'r engage,
> Yet neither *Charles* nor *James* be in a Rage?
> And I not strip the Gilding off a Knave,
> Un-plac'd, un-pension'd, no Man's Heir, or Slave?
> I will, or perish in the gen'rous Cause.
>
> (111–17)

What we have here is both the proud personal reaffirmation of the laureate tradition and what appears to be a radical reinterpretation of its whole basis. Although he has been reluctantly forced into this view, Pope seems to be saying that the poet no longer needs the traditional upper-class supports and sanctions. Instead of being the spokesman for the laws, the poet must become the lawgiver and punisher himself, for the laws are now in abeyance:

> Hear this and tremble! you, who 'scape the Laws.
> Yes, while I live, no rich or noble knave
> Shall walk the World, in credit, to his grave.
>
> (118–20)

Influenced by Swift and the long rule of Walpole, Pope's political disaffection and pessimism have deepened. For some time,
negative connotations of the word "polite" and suggestions of
false politeness have come increasingly to be associated not only
with individuals but with the whole upper-class world. Timon's
chaplain "never mentions hell to ears polite," and Sir Balaam:

> . . . marries, bows at Court, and grows polite,
> Leaves the dull Cits, and joins (to please the fair)
> The well-bred cuckolds in St. James' air.
> ("Epistle to Bathurst," 386–88, p. 586)

Pope himself contrasts his attack on the "whole polite world" in
the 1742 *Dunciad* with his 1728 attack on the "Dunces of a lower
Species."[29] The earlier books are concerned with a threat to the
polite world. But in 1742 it is the radical corruption of the polite
world that is itself the problem, and satire on aristocratic education and irresponsibility has become central. Pope is drawing
increasingly on Bolingbroke's anti-Walpole analysis of British
corruption and on the whole attack on luxurious politeness in
The Craftsman—the comparison with Periclean Athens, for example, where the "extravagant and unnatural flow of the public
money by degrees introduced that spirit of expense and luxury
amongst all men under the mistaken notion of politeness."[30]
Politeness therefore alters in signification as Pope's ideological
purposes apparently change. He seems to be recognizing the
breakdown of his ideological attempt to blend the old and the
new, controlling the energies of commercialism and capitalism
by a modified version of the old sanctions as the poet of mores.
Politeness has been spoilt by the "corrupt & corruptible world
within the vortex of the Town & Court."[31] It is now an amoral
luxury, the product of a false art, and the symptom of a false
civilization. To be polite at all in such a society is no longer a
viable option, and Pope underlines this, of course, by attributing
the praise of Horace's "sly, polite, insinuating Stile," which
"could please at Court, and make AUGUSTUS smile" (Dialogue
1. 19–20, p. 688) to the false "friend" of the "Epilogue to the
Satires."

All this makes the problem of the satirist's authority an urgent
one, however. It is one thing to attack contemporary aristocrats
and courtiers, as Ben Jonson had done, by their own ideal norms.
But Jonson draws his authority partly from that upper class,
legitimized themselves precisely because they recognize the
same norms and thus license Jonson to remind them of them. It is

another thing altogether to imply that the whole upper class is irredeemably corrupt. For where then will Pope draw that elite audience that the whole orientation of his poetry demands, and by what standards can he educate them? Is his authority drawn solely from an idealized past, and if so then how can these standards be made to seem viable in the contemporary world? Are they the standards of a small, uncorrupted minority, or is Pope now their sole embodiment as well as their sole spokesman?

> Yes, the last Pen for Freedom let me draw,
> When Truth stands trembling on the edge of Law:
> Here, Last of *Britons!* let your Names be read;
> Are none, none living? let me praise the Dead,
> And for that Cause which made your Fathers shine,
> Fall, by the Votes of their degen'rate Line!
> ("Epilogue to the Satires," Dialogue 2. 248–53, p. 703)

There is no doubting Pope's real political and social pessimism at this time, to which his letters also testify. But he leaves the questions about the satirist's authority unanswered as part of a deliberate process of mystification rather than admitting he cannot answer them. He takes the "honest muse" to its ultimate extreme of apparently rejecting society altogether and claiming to be the only good man left.[32] Yet an audience is still powerfully implicit in these poems, and so are standards of politeness that have a degree of general acceptance. Satire increasingly now involves engagement not only with vulgarity but also with real moral evil. In the "Epistle to Dr. Arbuthnot" he deliberately rejects the polite cautions of Arbuthnot in order to "flap this Bug with gilded wings." But the very recognition of the presence of the censor, Arbuthnot, remains a kind of testimony that Pope is not going outside the bounds of politeness unawares. In the "Epilogue to the Satires," as Thomas R. Edwards points out, the satiric *adversarius*, the "friend," is Pope too, but "in him are punished just those elements of civilized personality which necessarily yet tragically thwart the full realisation of one's best impulses," all the "defences of urbane, ironic civility."[33] Once again, however, although the poem is much more radical than the "Epistle to Dr. Arbuthnot," the presence of the "friend" and all his specious arguments provides Pope's implicit justification for the stance he is taking. Pope's "filthy Simile" is as shocking as possible, but it remains different from Swift's use of similar devices in that Pope's own recognition of how shocking but nevertheless essential it is built into the poem.

Pope's reinterpretation of the laureate tradition is actually less radical than it may appear, or rather, perhaps, he disguises both from himself and his readers the full implications of his need to alter its class basis. His pessimism itself contains a considerable degree of rhetorical exaggeration, and his rhetorical control helps him avoid, for example, what many critics have considered to be the unsatisfactory elements of the last part of the "Verses on the Death of Dr. Swift."[34] If all he ultimately has to oppose to corruption is a purely personal achievement and a purely personal defiance, as he sometimes asserts, then at other times he disguises the fact well. For Pope remains adept at surrounding his dictates with the authority of ancient sanctions, although he is in reality creating the impression of a whole framework out of what are no more than surviving fragments. He uses orthodox Christianity in the fourth book of The Dunciad, for example, mainly as a weapon to attack the heresy and freethinking of the new age. He draws elsewhere on the abstract authority of "Virtue" while knowing full well that it has been coopted into a party political campaign.[35]

If in one way then Pope comes to recognize the failure of his great ideological enterprise, in another sense he never gives up on it. It might be possible to read the emphasis on silence at the end of the "Epilogue to the Satires" and the fourth book of The Dunciad as some final tragic contradiction—the need to continue the ideological struggle and the simultaneous recognition of its impossibility. But this would be melodramatic. Pope's ideological struggle, with which his sense of the role of the poet is totally bound up, has become more and more paradoxical and inverted. He has not been able to freeze the social developments of his time and impose an ancient morality and a preconceived class armature upon capitalism. His authority has become divorced not only from its court place but even from its traditional class basis. Yet Pope preserves the outlines of the traditional ethos at the same time as he rejects it. The fourth book of The Dunciad keeps the framework of the laureate poet's theme of the education of the nobility, combining it with the Renaissance-humanist and Scriblerian tradition of the parody of learning in order to describe what has gone wrong. It is witty, satiric, and ironically inverted, and is thus differentiated from the false elevations of modern epic. On the other hand, of course, as Aubrey Williams was the first to point out, it attains to a genuine epic seriousness and profundity of its own too.[35] It is not, like Swift's "On Poetry: A Rapsody" simply an *inversion* of the mores tradition.

For the "Pope" who absolutely rejects his society *within* these final poems is a kind of persona or satiric device, used by Pope, the poet outside the poems, in the same way as Swift uses Gulliver's rejection of mankind. The rejection is heartfelt, but not the whole story. It remains rhetorical, a last-ditch, eleventh-hour reassertion of the responsibility of the public poet and commentator on mores, rather than its abnegation. Pope images at the end of the "Epilogue to the Satires", Dialogue 1 and even more in *Dunciad* 4 a final catastrophe: the complete breaking forth of all the energies of capitalism, consumerism, profit, and self-interest from the traditional constraints. But by writing as if the final catastrophe has already occurred, Pope is still trying to stir up the righteous indignation of his readers and thus, like the makers of films on the nuclear holocaust, prevent it from happening.

In refusing to give up the laureate poet's responsibility over mores, Pope is refusing to give up his attempt to control and channel the new developments into conservative directions. At the same time, though, it is impossible not to admire his increasingly desperate determination that manners, ethics, politics, and poetry should not be split off from each other.

Notes

Introduction

1. J. H. Plumb, *England in the Eighteenth Century* (Harmondsworth: Penguin Books, 1950; reprint, 1968), p. 33.

2. John Cannon, *Aristocratic Century: the Peerage of Eighteenth-Century England* (Cambridge: University Press, 1984); J. C. D. Clark, *English Society, 1688–1832: Ideology, Social Structure and Political Practice during the Ancien Régime* (Cambridge: University Press, 1985).

3. See Claude Lévi-Strauss, *Tristes tropique*, trans. John Russell (New York: Criterion Books, 1961), p. 391; Brean Hammond summarizes the point nicely in *Pope* (Brighton: Harvester Press, 1986), p. 151.

4. Terry Eagleton, *Literary Theory, An Introduction* (Oxford: Blackwell, 1983), p. 15, reprinted with other useful material, by Victor Lee in *English Literature in Schools: Exploring the Curriculum* (Milton Keynes: Open University Press, 1987), pp. 15–16. For general treatments see Raymond Williams, *Keywords: A Vocabulary of Culture and Society* (London: Croom Helm and Fontana, 1976), pp. 126–30; and David McLellan, *Ideology* (Milton Keynes: Open University Press, 1987).

5. Pierre Bourdieu, *Outline of a Theory of Practice*, trans. R. Nice (Cambridge: University Press, 1977), pp. 94–95, cited by Peter Stallybrass and Allon White in *The Politics and Poetics of Transgression* (London: Methuen, 1986), p. 88.

6. Thorstein Veblen, *The Theory of the Leisure Class* (London: Allen and Unwin, 1925), pp. 48–49. See also Leonore Davidoff, *The Best Circles* (1973; reprint, London: Cresset Books, 1986).

7. Norbert Elias, *The Civilising Process* (1939; reprint, Oxford: Basil Blackwell, 1978).

8. Aristotle, *Politics* 3.13, cited in Cannon, *Aristocratic Century*, p. 35; C. E. Chaffin, "The Two Cities: Christian and Pagan Literary Styles in Rome," *The Classical World*, ed. David Daiches and Anthony Thorlby (London: Aldus Books, 1972), p. 463; Mason Hammond, *The City in the Ancient World* (Cambridge: Harvard University Press, 1972), p. 181.

9. D. S. Brewer, "Class Distinction in Chaucer," *Speculum* 43 (1968): 290–305; Homai Shrof, *The Eighteenth Century Novel: The Idea of the Gentleman* (London: Edward Arnold, 1979), pp. 19–20. See too Michael McKeon, *The Origins of the English Novel, 1600–1740* (London and Baltimore: Johns Hopkins University Press, 1987), p. 131.

10. Chaucer, "The Clerks Tale," 206–7, *Works*, ed. F. N. Robinson (Cambridge, Mass.: Riverside Press, 1961), p. 103; *Institucion of a Gentleman* (1555), cited in Humphrey Tonkin, *Spenser's Courteous Pastoral* (Oxford: Clarendon Press, 1972), note 2, p. 160; John B. Morrall, *The Medieval Imprint* (Harmondsworth: Penguin Books, 1970), pp. 107–14; for the most recent and fullest

treatment see Maurice Keen, *Chivalry* (New Haven: Yale University Press, 1984). See too George Vogt, "Gleanings of the History of a Sentiment," *Journal of English and Germanic Philology* 24 (1925): 105–25. The Pauline text is 1 Cor. 1:26 in *The Jerusalem Bible* (London: Darton, Longman and Todd, 1966), p. 293.

11. Castiglione, *The Book of the Courtier*, trans. Hoby (London: Dent, 1928) pp. 43–44, cited in Anthea Hume, *Edmund Spenser, Protestant Poet* (Cambridge: University Press, 1984), p. 142.

12. *A Dictionary of the English Language*, 6th ed. (1785); Lawrence Manley, *Convention, 1500–1750* (Cambridge: Harvard University Press, 1980).

13. Domna Stanton, *The Aristocrat as Art: A Study of the Honnête Homme and the Dandy in Seventeenth- and Nineteenth-Century French Literature* (New York: Columbia University Press, 1980), p. 132.

14. Lawrence Klein, "The Third Earl of Shaftesbury and the Progress of Politeness," *Eighteenth-Century Studies* 18 (1984–85): 186–214; J. G. A. Pocock, most recently in *Virtue, Commerce and History: Essays on Political Thought and History, Chiefly in the Eighteenth Century* (Cambridge: University Press, 1986), pp. 48–49, 115; Neil McKendrick, John Brewer, and J. H. Plumb, *The Birth of a Consumer Society: The Commercialization of Eighteenth-Century England* (London: Hutchinson, 1984).

15. Jürgen Habermas, *Strukturwändel der Öffentlichkeit* (Berlin: Neuwied, Luchterhand, 1962); P. U. Hohendahl, *The Institution of Criticism* (Ithaca: Cornell University Press, 1982); T. Eagleton, *The Function of Criticism: The Spectator to Post-Structuralism* (London: Verso, 1984) pp. 9–27; Patrick Parrinder, *The Failure of Theory: Essays on Criticism of Contemporary Fiction* (Brighton: Harvester, (1987), pp. 35–36; E. P. Thompson, "Patrician Society, Plebeian Culture," *Journal of Social History* 7 (1974): 382–405.

16. William Empson, *Some Versions of Pastoral* (London: Chatto and Windus, 1935), p. 236.

17. Fr. John Constable, *The Conversation of Gentlemen*, (1738), cited by Peter Dixon, *The World of Pope's Satires* (London: Methuen, 1968), p. 14. For good brief discussions of the overlap between literary decorum and social pressures see Manley, *Convention*, pp. 37–39 and Walter Jackson Bate, *The Burden of the Past and the English Poet* (London: Chatto and Windus, 1971), pp. 18–21.

18. John Dennis, *Critical Works*, ed. E. N. Hooker (Baltimore: Johns Hopkins Press, 1939) 2, cxiii and 497.

Chapter 1. The "Courtier's Claim and the Citt's Ambition": Eighteenth-Century Versions of Politeness

1. See Williams, *Keywords*, pp. 51–59; E. P. Thompson, "Eighteenth-Century English Society: Class Struggle without Class?" *Social History* 3(1978): 133–65; R. S. Neale, *Class in English History, 1600–1850* (Oxford: Blackwell, 1981). The clearest summary of the arguments is in W. A. Speck, *Society and Literature in England, 1700–1760* (Dublin: Gill and Macmillan, 1983), pp. 42–45.

2. Lawrence Stone, *An Open Elite? England 1540–1880* (Oxford: Clarendon Press, 1984). Cannon, *Aristocratic Century*; Clark, *English Society, 1688–1832*. E. P. Thompson, "Patrician Society, Plebeian Culture," *Journal of Social History* 7(1974): 382–405; McKeon, *Origins of English Novel*, p. 167.

3. Lawrence Stone, "Social Mobility in England, 1500–1700," *Past and Present* 33(1966): 15–16.

4. Sir Thomas Smith, *De Republica Anglorum* (1612), ed. L. Alston (Cambridge: University Press, 1906), pp. 39–40, first cited by Michael Shinagel, *Defoe and Middle-Class Gentility* (Cambridge: Harvard University Press, 1968), p. 227. See too John Mason, *Gentlefolk in the Making* (Philadelphia: University Press, 1953).

5. V. B. Heltzel, "Chesterfield and the Tradition of the Ideal Gentleman," (Ph.D. dissertation, University of Chicago, 1925). For other valuable studies of eighteenth-century politeness see Shrof, *Eighteenth-Century Novel: The Idea of the Gentleman*; John Barrell, *An Equal Wide Survey, English Literature in History* (London: Hutchinson, 1983); McKendrick, Brewer, and Plumb, *Birth of a Consumer Society*; C. J. Rawson, "Gentlemen and Dancing Masters: Thoughts on Fielding, Chesterfield and the Genteel," *Eighteenth-Century Studies* 1(1967–68): 127–58. See too David Castronovo, *The English Gentleman: Image and Ideals in Literature and Society* (New York: Ungar, 1987).

6. McKendrick, Brewer, and Plumb, *Birth of a Consumer Society*; Shaftesbury, "Letter Concerning Design" (1712), cited by Michael Foss, *The Age of Patronage: The Arts in Society, 1660–1750* (London: Hamish Hamilton, 1971), p. 199; Leonard Welsted, "Dissertation Concerning the Perfection of the English Language, the State of Poetry etc." (1724), cited by Daniel A. Fineman, "Leonard Welsted: Gentleman Poet of the Augustan Age," (Ph.D. dissertation, University of Pennsylvania, 1950), p. 73.

7. Lord Tyrconnel, speaking in the House of Lords, cited by George Rudé, *Hanoverian London 1714–1818* (London: Secker and Warburg, 1971), p. 135. I owe this reference to Stephen Copley.

8. For the "pseudo-gentry" see Alan Everitt, "Social Mobility in Early Modern England," *Past and Present* 33 (1966): 70–71. The phrase "the politer Part of Mankind" is a common one, used, for example, by Isaac Watts in the preface to his *Hymns and Spiritual Songs*, cited by David Morris, *The Religious Sublime* (Lexington: Kentucky University Press, 1972), p. 106. See too Nicholas Rogers, "Money, Land and Lineage: the Big Bourgeoisie of Hanoverian London," *Social History* 4(1979): 449; Shaftesbury, *Characteristics of Men, Manners, Opinions, Times*, ed. John M. Robertson (Indianapolis: Bobbs-Merrill, 1964), 1:84

9. Daniel Defoe, *Moll Flanders*, ed. G. A. Starr (London: Oxford University Press, 1971), p. 60. See W. A. Speck, *Stability and Strife: England 1714–1760* (London: Edward Arnold, 1977), p. 54; Voltaire cited by Derek Jarrett, *England in the Age of Hogarth* (London: Hart-Davis, MacGibbon, 1974), p. 15.

10. Cited by E. Neville Williams, *Life in Georgian England* (London: Batsford, 1962), p. 73.

11. The phrase "Genteel Mania" comes from *The World* (1756), cited by Jarrett, *Hogarth*, p. 193; Bolingbroke, *Works* (Philadelphia, 1841), 2:165. I owe this reference to D. J. Hudson "Pope, Bolingbroke and *The Craftsman* (Ph.D. dissertation, Reading, 1978), p. 100.

12. Stone, "Social Mobility," p. 55.

13. Maurice Magendie, *La Politesse Mondaine et les Théories de L'honnêteté en France, au XVIIe Siècle de 1600–1660*, 2 vols. (Paris: Alcan, 1926); Stanton, *Aristocrat as Art*.

14. Guy Miege, "The Present State of Great Britain" (1748), in *Aristocratic Government and Society in Eighteenth-Century England*, ed. Daniel Baugh (New York: Franklin Watts, 1975), p. 47. *The Letters of Philip Dormer Stanhope, Fourth Earl of Chesterfield*, ed. Bonamy Dobrée (1932; reprint, 6 vols., New

York, A. M. S. Press, 1968) No. 1774, 16 May 1751, 4:1730–31, cited by Rawson, *Eighteenth-Century Studies* 1(1967–68): 152.

15. Bishop Sprat, "Life of Cowley," cited in Dixon, *The World of Pope's Satires*, p. 44; *The Diary of Dudley Ryder*, ed. William Matthews (London: Methuen, 1968), p. 217.

16. *The Spectator*, No. 119, ed. D. F. Bond (Oxford: Clarendon Press, 1965), 1:486–87.

17. Stallybrass and White, *Politics and Poetics of Transgression*, p. 97.

18. Henry Fielding, *Joseph Andrews*, ed. Martin Battestin (Oxford: Clarendon Press, 1967), pp. 217–18, cited in Rawson, *Eighteenth-Century Studies* 1:149; E. P. Thompson, "Patrician Society, Plebeian Culture," *Journal of Social History* 7(1974):382–405; Cannon, *Aristocratic Century*, p. ix; Roy Porter, "The Enlightenment in England," *The Enlightenment in National Context*, ed. Porter and M. Teich (Cambridge: University Press, 1981), p. 10.

19. Sir Lewis Namier, "The Social Foundations," ed. Baugh, in *Aristocratic Government*, p. 214; Shaftesbury, *Characteristics*, 1:46.

20. Chesterfield, *Letters*, ed. Dobrée, No. 1599, 4:1252, cited by Richard Sennet in *The Fall of Public Man* (Cambridge: University Press, 1974), p. 62. C. J. Rawson, *Henry Fielding and the Augustan Ideal under Stress* (London: Routledge and Kegan Paul, 1972), p. 19.

21. Roy Porter, *English Society in the Eighteenth Century*, (Harmondsworth: Pelican, 1982), p. 33; Stallybrass and White, *Politics and Poetics of Transgression*, p. 107; R. W. Malcolmson, *Popular Recreations in English Society, 1700–1850* (Cambridge: University Press, 1973).

22. John Sekora, *Luxury: The Concept in Western Thought, Eden to Smollett* (Baltimore: Johns Hopkins University Press, 1977).

23. Klein, "Progress of Politeness."

24. Stephen Copley, introduction to *Literature and the Social Order in Eighteenth-Century England* (Beckenham: Croom Helm, 1984); Pocock, *Virtue, Commerce and History*, 49; Mark Goldie, "The rise of politeness" (review of *Virtue, Commerce and History* by Pocock, *Times Literary Supplement*, 27 June 1986, p. 715. Aaron Hill to Thompson, 7 Feb. 1735, cited in Bonamy Dobrée, "The Theme of Patriotism in Poetry of the Early Eighteenth Century, 1700–1740," *Proceedings of the British Academy* 35(1949): 61.

25. For a background study see Isaac Kramnick, *Bolingbroke and his Circle: The Politics of Nostalgia in the Age of Walpole* (Cambridge: Harvard University Press, 1968). For civic humanism see J. G. A. Pocock, *The Machiavellian Moment: Florentine Political Thought and the Atlantic Republican Tradition* (Princeton: Princeton University Press, 1977).

26. George A. Brauer, Jr., "Good Breeding in the Eighteenth Century," *University of Texas Studies in English* 32(1953):25–44; John Arbuthnot, *John Bull Still in his Senses* (1712), cited by Robert Steensma, *Dr. John Arbuthnot* (Boston: Twayne, 1979), p. 61.

27. Lawrence Stone, *The Family, Sex and Marriage in England, 1500–1800* (London: Weidenfeld and Nicolson, 1977), chap. 6. For sincerity see Rachel Trickett, *The Honest Muse: A Study in Augustan Verse* (Oxford: Clarendon Press, 1967); Leon Guilhamet, *The Sincere Ideal: Studies in Sincerity in Eighteenth-Century Literature* (Montreal and London: McGill-Queens University Press, 1974); Lionel Trilling, *Sincerity and Authenticity* (London: Oxford University Press, 1972).

28. Jeremy Collier, *A Short View of the Immorality and Profaneness of the English Stage* (London, 1698), p. 143.

29. Cited by H. N. Fairchild, *Religious Trends in English Poetry* (New York: Columbia University Press, 1939) 1:80.

30. T. A. Curtis and W. A. Speck, "The Societies for the Reformation of Manners: A Case History in the Theory and Practice of Moral Reform," *Literature and History* 3(1976): 45–64.

31. For comments on the growth of prudery see A. S. Collins, "The Growth of the Reading Public during the Eighteenth Century," *Review of English Studies* 2(1926): 431, where the *Scots Magazine* remark is cited.

32. Stone, *Family, Sex and Marriage*, p. 257; *Pamela* (Oxford: Basil Blackwell, 1929)2:78.

33. Alice Clark, *Working Life of Women in the Seventeenth Century* (London: Routledge, 1919.

34. John Glanvil, *Poems Consisting of Originals and Translations* (1725), cited by Fairchild, *Religious Trends* 1:18.

35. Ellen Pollak, *The Poetics of Sexual Myth: Gender and Ideology in the Verse of Swift and Pope* (Chicago: University of Chicago Press, 1985), p. 26; Katharine M. Rogers, *The Troublesome Helpmate: A History of Misogyny in Literature* (Seattle: University of Washington Press, 1966), p. 174.

36. James Thomson, *The Seasons*, ed. James Sambrook (Oxford: The Clarendon Press, 1981), "Autumn," 576–85, 603–9, pp. 166, 168.

37. Dedication to *The Spectator*, ed. Bond, 5:174.

38. Maximillian E. Novak, introduction to Edward and Lillian D. Bloom, Edward Leites, *Educating the Audience: Addison and Steele and Eighteenth Century Culture* (Los Angeles: Clark Memorial Library, 1984), p. 6.

39. Lee Andrew Elioseff, "Joseph Addison's Political Animal," *Eighteenth-Century Studies* 6(1973):373.

40. Stallybrass and White, *Politics and Poetics of Transgression*, p. 83.

41. *The Guardian*, ed. John Calhoun Stephens (Lexington: University of Kentucky Press, 1983), No. 21, p. 104.

42. Eliopsepf, p. 379; *The Tatler*, No. 5, ed. Donald F. Bond (Oxford: The Clarendon Press, 1987), I, 48.

43. "Argument against Abolishing of Christianity," *Prose Works*, ed. Herbert Davis, 14 vols. (Oxford: Blackwell, 1957–68), 2:27–28.

Chapter 2. "This Potent School of Manners": Politics, the Poet, and Mores

1. John Dryden, dedication to the *Aeneid* (1697), *The Poems of John Dryden*, ed. James Kinsley (Oxford: Clarendon Press, 1958), 3: 1053.

2. "To the Reader Concerning the Vertues of an Heroique Poem," (1675), ed. J. E. Spingarn in *Critical Essays of the Seventeenth Century* (1908–9); reprint, Bloomington: Indiana University Press, 1957), 2: 68.

3. *Diary*, ed. Matthews, p. 78.

4. Samuel Wesley, *Epistle to a Friend Concerning Poets* (London, 1700), 131–34.

5. J. W. Saunders, "The Stigma of Print," *Essays in Criticism* 1(1959):139–64. Robert Folkenflik, "Patronage and the Poet-Hero," *Huntingdon Library Quarterly* 48 (1985): 363–79.

6. Charles Montagu, "An Epistle to Charles, Earl of Dorset Occasioned by his Majesty's Victory in Ireland, 1690," in *Works of the English Poets*, ed.

Alexander Chalmers (London, 1810), 9:31.

7. Thomas Seldfield, *The Compleat Gentleman* (London, 1730), cited by Heltzel, "Chesterfield," p. 168.

8. *Poems of Anne Countess of Winchelsea*, ed. Myra Reynolds (Chicago: University of Chicago Press, 1903), 74–83, p. 193.

9. *Literary Works of Matthew Prior*, ed. Monroe K. Spears and George Bunker Wright (Oxford: Clarendon Press, 1959), 1:247.

10. For the debate about positive and negative images of Horace in the period see Howard Weinbrot, *Augustus Caesar in "Augustan" England* (Princeton: Princeton University Press, 1978), p. 217 and Howard Erskine-Hill, *The Augustan Idea in English Literature* (London: Edward Arnold, 1983), p. 308. The comment about the revolutionary quality of the earlier seventeenth century is from Michael McKeon, *Origins*, p. 269.

11. Richard Helgerson, *Self-Crowned Laureates: Spenser, Jonson, Milton and the Literary System* (Berkeley and Los Angeles: University of California Press, 1983).

12. J. W. Saunders, "The Social Situation of Seventeenth Century Poetry," in *Metaphysical Poetry*, Stratford-upon-Avon Studies 2, ed. Malcolm Bradbury and John Palmer (London: Edward Arnold, 1970), p. 247.

13. *Poems of Alexander Pope*, ed. Maynard Mack (London: Methuen, 1967), 9:4–5.

14. Sir William Davenant, preface to *Gondibert*, ed. David F. Gladish (Oxford: Clarendon Press, 1971), p. 38.

15. Ben Jonson, *Works*, 11 vols., ed. C. H. Herford and P. Simpson (Oxford: Clarendon Press, 1925–52) 5:17; W. L. Cherniak, "The Heroic Occasional Poem: Panegyric and Satire in the Restoration," *Modern Language Quarterly* 26(1965): 523–35.

16. "A Letter of the Author's," *The Fairie Queene*, ed. A. C. Hamilton (London: Longmans, 1977), p. 737.

17. "Epistle to Katherine, Lady Aubigny," 49–50, in Jonson, *Works*, ed. Herford and Simpson, 8:118.

18. Dedication and *Cynthia's Revels* 5,1,30–37 in Jonson, *Works*, ed. Herford and Simpson, 4:131–32. My comments on Jonson deal, of course, only with one aspect of his work and attitudes. For a subtle discussion of Jonson's ideological attitudes see Don E. Wayne, *Penshurst: The Semiotics of Place and the Poetics of History* (London: Methuen, 1984). See too Peter Womack, *Ben Jonson: Rereading Literature* (Oxford: Blackwell, 1987).

19. P. W. Thomas, "Two Cultures? Court and Country under Charles," in *The Origins of the English Civil War*, ed. Conrad Russell (London: Macmillan, 1973), p. 175. Martin Butler, *Theatre and Crisis, 1632–1642* (Cambridge: University Press, 1984) has reminded us not to exaggerate the court's cultural decline.

20. *Poems of Edmund Waller*, ed. G. B. Thorn Drury (London: Routledge, 1905), 1:12; W. L. Cherniak, *The Poetry of Limitation: A Study of Edmund Waller* (New Haven: Yale University Press, 1968), p. 206.

21. "To the Duchess," Thorn Drury 2:71; Cherniak, p. 143.

22. "To his Noble Friend Mr. Richard Lovelace, upon his Poems," cited in Annabel M. Patterson, *Marvell and the Civic Crown* (Princeton: Princeton University Press, 1978), p. 18.

23. Helgerson, *Self-crowned Laureates*, p. 280.

24. "An Allusion to Horace," *The Poems of John Wilmot, Earl of Rochester* ed. Keith Walker (Oxford: Blackwell, 1984), p. 101; Stallybrass and White, *Politics*

and Poetics of Transgression, pp. 100–101.

25. Donald Hanson, *From Kingdom to Commonwealth: The Development of Civic Consciousness in English Political Thought* (Cambridge: Harvard University Press, 1970). See too W. H. Greenleaf, *Order, Empiricism and Politics: Two Traditions of English Political Thought, 1500–1700* (Oxford: University Press, 1964); J. C. D. Clark, *English Society, 1688–1832.*

26. Dedication to "Georgics" (1697), *Poems of John Dryden,* ed. Kinsley, 2:916.

27. Alan Robinson, "Swift and Renaissance Poetry: A Declaration of Independence," *British Journal for Eighteenth-Century Studies* 8 (1985): 37–49.

28. "Discourse Concerning the Origin and Progress of Satire," *Poems,* ed. Kinsley, 2:617.

29. Dedication to *Familiar Letters of Love, Gallantry and Several Occasions by the Wits of the Past and Present Age* (London, 1718).

30. See W. J. Courthope, *A History of English Poetry,* vol. 5 (London: Macmillan, 1925), chap. 2; C. A. Moore, "Whig Panegyric Verse, 1700–1760," *PMLA* 41(1926):362–401; Bonamy Dobrée, "The Theme of Patriotism in the Poetry of the Early Eighteenth Century, *Proceedings of the British Academy* 35 (1949): 49–65.

31. Preface to *A Paraphrase on the Book of Job* (1700), cited in Harry M. Solomon, *Sir Richard Blackmore* (Boston: Wayne, 1980), p. 85.

32. Sir Richard Blackmore, *Prince Arthur,* cited in Solomon, *Blackmore,* pp. 42–43.

33. *Seasons,* ed. Sambrook, "Spring," 67, p. 6.

34. Barrell, *English Literature in History: An Equal Wide Survey,* pp. 50–90; *Liberty, The Castle of Indolence and Other Poems,* ed. James Sambrook (Oxford: Clarendon Press, 1986), 2.279 and 5.671–3, pp. 65, 145.

35. James Thompson, *Letters and Documents,* ed. A. D. McKillp (Lawrence: University of Kansas Press, 1958), p. 105, cited in Ralph Cohen, *The Unfolding of "The Seasons"* (London: Routledge and Kegan Paul, 1970), p. 286.

36. O. H. K. Spate, "The Muse of Mercantilism: Jago, Grainger and Dyer," in *Studies in the Eighteenth Century,* ed. R. F. Brissenden (Canberra: Australian National University Press, 1968). For a careful analysis see W. A. Speck, *Literature and Society in the Eighteenth Century,* pp. 33, 65.

37. Thomas Blackwell, *Enquiry into the Life and Writings of Homer* (1735). See W. J. Bate, *Burden of the Past,* p. 49–50.

38. Michael McKeon, *Origins.*

39. *Tatler,* No. 244 (1710 ed.), p. 311.

40. William Whitehead, "On Ridicule" (1743), cited by Ramon Selden, *English Verse Satire* (London: Allen and Unwin, 1978), p. 165.

41. John Pomfret, "The Choice," in *The Oxford Book of Eighteenth Century Verse,* ed. D. Nichol Smith (Oxford: Clarendon Press, 1926), p. 3.

42. John Oldmixon, *Poems on Several Occasions* (London, 1696).

43. In Chalmers, *English Poets,* 8:403.

44. "The Vision," in Chalmers, *English Poets,* 9:26.

45. In "A Receipt for the Vapours," for example. See Katharine Rogers, *Troublesome Helpmate,* p. 174.

46. "To the Immortal Memory of Mr. Edmund Waller," in Chalmers, 11:13.

47. Joseph Spence, *Observations, Anecdotes and Characters of Books and Men,* ed. James Osborn (Oxford: Clarendon Press, 1966), 1:32; "Epistle to Dr. Arbuthnot," 135–36, p. 602.

Chapter 3. "Alike Fantastick, If Too New, or Old": Politeness and the Dilemma of Traditional Poets

1. Frances M. Rippy, *Matthew Prior* (Boston: Twayne, 1986), pp. 122–31.

2. W. A. Speck, *Society and Literature in England, 1700–1760* (Dublin: Gill and Macmillan, 1983), p. 27; J. A. Downie, review of *Swift's Tory Politics* by F. P. Lock in *Eighteenth-Century Studies* 19 (1985): 113–15.

3. Pocock, *Machiavellian Moment.*

4. Swift, *Poetical Works,* ed. Herbert Davis (Oxford: Clarendon Press, 1967), "On Poetry: A Rapsody," 186, p. 574.

5. C. J. Rawson, *Order from Confusion Sprung: Studies in Eighteenth-Century Literature from Swift to Cowper* (London: Allen and Unwin, 1985), p. 257.

6. "Hints towards an Essay on Conversation," in *Prose Works* 4:94.

7. Mckeon, *Origins,* p. 154.

8. "Strephon and Chloe," 271–73 in *Poetical Works.*

9. Margaret Doody, review of *Alexander Pope* by Laura Brown, *The Scriblerian* 19(1987): 180.

10. *The Correspondence of Alexander Pope,* ed. George Sherburn (Oxford: Clarendon Press, 1956), 3:52.

11. Speck, *Society and Literature,* pp. 35, 65.

12. Bertrand A. Goldgar, *Walpole and the Wits: The Relation of Politics to Literature, 1722–1742* (Lincoln, Nebr.: University of Nebraska Press, 1976), p. 34.

13. *The Poems of Alexander Pope,* ed. John Butt (London: Methuen, 1963), p. xxvii.

14. Roscommon, "Essay on Translated Verse," in *Critical Essays of the Seventeenth Century,* ed. J. E. Spingarn, 2:306.

15. Giles Jacob, *An Historical Account of the Lives and Writings of Our Most Considerable English Poets* (London, 1720), p. xix, cited by David Morris, *The Religious Sublime,* p. 25. For a discussion of the inhibiting effects of "great poetry" on the poets of the period see Austin Warren, *Rage for Order* (Chicago: University of Chicago Press, 1948), pp. 39–40. See too W. J. Bate, *Burden of the Past.* Marshall Brown ("The Urbane Sublime," *ELH* 45 (1978): 236–54) shows that the distinction between sublime and satirical poets should not be exaggerated, but Pope's strategies remain very different from those of the poets Brown discusses.

16. Louis I. Bredvold, "The Gloom of the Tory Satirists," in *Eighteenth-Century English Literature: Modern Essays in Criticism,* ed. James L. Clifford (New York: Oxford University Press, 1959), pp. 3–20.

17. James Sutherland, *A Preface to Eighteenth-Century Poetry* (London: Oxford University Press, 1963), p. 81.

18. C. J. Rawson, *Order from Confusion Sprung,* p. 287.

19. R. Kraft, "Class Analysis of a Literary Controversy: Wit and Sense in Seventeenth-Century English Literature," *Science and Society* 10 (1946):80–92; E. N. Hooker, "Pope on Wit: The *Essay on Criticism,*" in *Eighteenth-Century English Literature,* ed. James Clifford (New York: Oxford University Press, 1959), pp. 42–61.

20. Ronald Paulson, *Popular and Polite Art in the Age of Hogarth and Fielding* (London and Notre Dame: University of Notre Dame Press, 1979), p. 133.

21. Stallybrass and White, *Transgression*, p. 107; *Correspondence* 4:382.
22. *Correspondence* 1:465.

Chapter 4. "Softest Manners, Gentlest Arts": The Polite Verse of Thomas Parnell

1. Pope, "Epistle to Robert Earl of Oxford, and Earl Mortimer," 4, p. 313; "Of Simplicity and Refinement in Writing," Hume, *Essays Moral, Political and Literary*, ed. T. Green and T. Grose, vol. 1 (London: Longman's 1898): 240–44; Goldsmith, "Life of Dr. Parnell" in *Works of Oliver Goldsmith*, ed. Arthur Friedman (Oxford: Clarendon Press, 1966) 3:407–428; Donald Davie, *Purity of Diction in English Verse* (London: Chatto and Windus, 1952), pp. 49, 139.
2. The volume as published in Dublin. See Pope, *Correspondence* 2:24; Spence, *Observations* 1:58; C. J. Rawson, "Swift's Certificate to Parnell's 'Posthumous Works'" *Modern Language Review* 57 (1962): 179–82. See too his "New Parnell Manuscripts," *Scriblerian* 1(1969):1–2.
3. Parnell, *Collected Poems of Thomas Parnell*, ed. Claude Rawson and F. P. Lock (Newark: University of Delaware Press, 1989), "Piety, Or, The Vision," 33, p. 294; "The Ecstasy," 83–86, p. 394. Parenthical references in the text henceforth are to this edition.
4. *The Critical Review*, August 1758, p. 121.
5. Richard Dircks, "Parnell's 'Batrachomuomachia' and the Homer Translation Controversy," *Notes and Queries* 201(1956): 339–42.
6. Reuben Brower, "Dryden and the Invention of Pope," in *Restoration and Eighteenth-Century Literature: Essays in Honour of A. D. Mckillop* (Chicago: Unviersity of Chicago Press, 1963), p. 212; Edmund Gosse, *A History of Eighteenth-Century English Literature* (London: Macmillan, 1889), pp. 136–37; Thomas Woodman, *Thomas Parnell* (Boston: Twayne, 1985).
7. "Simplicity and Refinement," *Essays*, p. 240.
8. Margaret C. Jacob, *The Newtonians and the English Constitution, 1689–1720* (Hassocks, Sussex: Harvester, 1976).
9. See R. D. Havens, "Parnell's "Hymn to Contentment," *Modern Language Notes* 59(1944):329–31.
10. *Catullus, Tibullus and Pervigilium Veneris*, ed. F. W. Cornish, J. P. Postage and J. W. Mackail (Cambridge: Harvard University Press, 1962), p. 351.
11. For an interesting comment by Leigh Hunt see Louis Landre, *Leigh Hunt* (Paris: Editions Belles Lettres, 1936), 2:493. 16
12. *Troublesome Helpmate*, p. 174. For discussion of Hesiod and other sources see Felicity A. Nussbaum, *The Brink of All We Hate: English Satires on Women, 1660–1750* (Lexington: University of Kentucky Press, 1984), pp. 136ff.
13. McKeon, *Origins*, p. 154.
14. *Spectator*, No. 419, ed. Bond, 3:570.
15. John Donne *The Satires, Epigrams and Verse Letters*, ed. W. Milgate (Oxford: Clarendon Press, 1967), 11–15, p. 11.
16. See A. P. Hudson, "The Hermit and Divine Providence," *Studies in Philology* 28(1931): 222–23.
17. Charles Peake, *Poetry of the Landscape and the Night* (London: Edward Arnold, 1967), p. 18.
18. See *Fairie Queene* 1.9.40.
19. Speck, *Society and Literature in England*, p. 41.

20. J. W. Draper, *The Funeral Elegy and the Rise of English Romanticism* (New York: New York University Press, 1929).

Chapter 5. "A Grace, a Manner, a Decorum": Matthew Prior's Polite Mystique

1. "Epitaph," 1:195; see too "The Old Gentry," 558, though this is of doubtful authenticity. References in the text are to *Literary Works of Matthew Prior*, ed. Monroe K. Spears and George Bunker Wright, 2 vols. (Oxford: Clarendon Press, 1959).

2. McKeon, *Origins*, p. 154.

3. See my article on Prior in the forthcoming *Spenser Encyclopaedia*.

4. W. B. Piper, *The Heroic Couplet* (Cleveland: Case Western Reserve University Press, pp. 119–20.

5. Sutherland, *Preface to Eighteenth Century Poetry*, p. 81.

6. Alex Preminger, *Encyclopaedia of Poetry and Poetics* (Princeton: Princeton University Press, 1965), p. 448.

7. For the most detailed account of the relations between Pope and Prior see Frances M. Rippy, "Matthew Prior and Alexander Pope: Their Personal and Literary Relationship" (Ph.D. Dissertation, Vanderbilt University, 1957). Some of the conclusions are summarized in the same author's *Matthew Prior* (Boston: Twayne, 1986).

8. Wright and Spears, 2:1034.

9. "Song," *Poems of John Wilmot, Earl of Rochester*, ed. Keith Walker, p. 39.

10. See Rachel Trickett, *The Honest Muse* (Oxford: Clarendon Press, 1967), p. 45; Ronald Rower, "Pastoral Wars: Prior's Poems to Chloe," *Ball State University Forum* 19(1978): 38–49.

11. Monroe K. Spears, "The Meaning of Prior's 'Alma,'" *English Literary History* 13(1946): 266–90; and "Ethical Aspects of Prior's Poetry," *Studies in Philology* 45(1948): 606–29.

Chapter 6. John Gay's "Due Civilities": The Ironies of Politeness

1. *The Beggar's Opera* 3.16 in John Gay, *Dramatic Works*, ed. John Fuller, 2 vols. (Oxford: Clarendon Press, 1983), 2:64. References to Gay's plays are henceforth to this edition.

2. John Gay, *Poetry and Prose*, ed. V. A. Dearing and C. Beckwith, 2 vols. (Oxford: Clarendon Press, 1947), 103–6, 1:132. References to Gay's poetry and prose are henceforth to this edition.

3. Patricia Spacks, *John Gay* (New York: Twayne, 1965), pp. 79–80. For a very nuanced account see the essay by Brean Hammond, "'A Poet and a Patron and Ten Pound': Patronage in Gay's Poetry," in *Gay and the Scriblerians*, ed. Nigel Wood and Peter Lewis (London: Vision Press, 1988; New York: St. Martin's Press, 1989).

4. "Epilogue," *Three Hours after Marriage*, *Dramatic Works*, 1:263.

5. Prologue to *The Captives*, 1:345.

6. *Letters of John Gay*, ed. C. F. Burgess (Oxford: Clarendon Press, 1966), p. 24.

7. Malcolmson, *Popular Recreations*, p. 68, cited in Stallybrass and White, *Transgression*, p. 86.

8. *The Present State of Wit* (London, 1711), *Poetry and Prose* 2:452.

9. Prologue to *The Captives*, 1:345; Spence, *Observations*, ed. Osburn, 1:106.

10. *Polly* 1.8, air 9, 2:87.

11. Alvin Kernan, *The Plot of Satire* (New Haven: Yale University Press, 1965) chap. 3, "The Magnifying Tendency," pp. 36–50.

12. See, for example, James Bramston, "The Man of Taste," in *A Collection of Poems*, ed. Robert Dodsley, 2d ed. (London, 1748), p. 292; see too Gerald Newman, *The Rise of English Nationalism: A Cultural History, 1740–1830* (London: Weidenfeld and Nicolson, 1987).

13. Spacks, *John Gay*, p. 79; see too Christine Rees, "Gay, Swift and the Nymphs of Drury Lane," *Essays in Criticism* 23(1973):12–14.

14. Empson, *Some Versions of Pastoral*, pp. 11–12.

15. Empson, p. 16.

16. Heidi Göbel, *Die Parodie der Englischen Hirtendichtung* (Heidelberg: C. Winter, 1982). See review by Bernfried Nugel in *The Scriblerian* 18(1986): 137.

17. John Barrell, *The Dark Side of the Landscape* (Cambridge: University Press, 1980), p. 58.

18. Empson, p. 230.

19. McKeon, *Origins*, p. 154.

20. Barrell, *Dark Side of the Landscape*, p. 55; "Gainsborough's Rural Vision," *The Listener* (12 May 1977), pp. 615–16.

21. Stephen Copley, "Luxury, Refuse and Poetry: John Gay's 'Trivia' " in *Gay and the Scriblerians* ed. Wood and Lewis. See also my own essay, " 'Vulgar Circumstance' and 'Due Civilities' " in this volume.

22. Sennet, *Fall of Public Man*, pp. 62, 84.

23. Copley, art. cit.

24. Paulson, *Popular and Polite Art*, p. 133.

25. Fable 2.31–34, 47–50, 2:384–85; Edwin Graham, "John Gay's Second Series, The Craftsman in the *Fables*," *Papers in Language and Literature* 5(1969):17–25.

Chapter 7. "A Kind of Artificial Good Sense": Swift and the Forms of Politeness

1. Swift, *Poetical Works*, ed. Herbert Davis (Oxford: Clarendon Press, 1967), "The Author upon Himself," 13–14, p. 148. References in the text to Swift's poetry are henceforth to this edition.

2. Swift, *Prose Works*, ed. Herbert Davis, 14 vols. (Oxford: Blackwell, 1939–68), "Intelligencer," No. 5, 12:40. References in the text to Swift's prose are henceforth to this edition.

3. "Hints Towards an Essay on Conversation," *Prose Works* 4:92.

4. "Hints towards an Essay on Conversation," *Prose Works* 4:94.

5. *Order from Confusion Sprung*, p. 55.

6. *Prose Works* 8:135.

7. *Prose Works* 3:10 and 150–51. See F. P. Lock, *Swift's Tory Politics* (London: Duckworth, 1983), pp. 174–78 and McKeon, *Origins*, pp. 169–70.

8. "On Good Manners and Good Breeding," *Prose Works* 4:214.

9. *Prose Works* 3:15, cited in J. A. Downie, *Jonathan Swift, Political Writer* (London: Routledge and Kegan Paul, 1984), p. 144.

10. "Hints Towards an Essay on Conversation," *Prose Works* 4:94.

11. *Correspondence* 1:117, cited for Basil Hall, "An Inverted Hypocrite: Swift the Churchman," in *The World of Jonathan Swift*, ed. Brian Vickers (Oxford: Basil Blackwell, 1968), p. 38.

12. *Prose Works* 4:249.

13. *Order*, p. 257.

14. *The Common Reader*, 2d ser., (London: Hogarth Press, 1935), p. 67.

15. *Prose Works* 4:94; Stallybrass and White, *Transgression*, p. 109.

16. Pollak, *Poetics of Sexual Myth*, pp. 179–80, for example.

17. For a helpful survey of the criticism see Nora Crow Jaffe, *The Poet Swift* (Hanover, N.H.: University of New England Press, 1977), pp. 102–20. Jae Num Lee, *Swift and Scatological Satire* (Albuquerque: University of New Mexico Press, 1971) remains the fullest account.

18. Elias, *The Civilising Process*.

19. Rawson, *Order*, pp. 164–65. See too Donald T. Siebert, "Swift's 'Fiat Odor': The Excremental Re-vision," in *Eighteenth-Century Studies* 19(1985): 21–38.

20. Davis, p. 185. Swift is here transforming a remark by Edward Bysshe in his *Art of English Poetry*, cited by Chester Chapin, *Personification in English Poetry* (New York: Kings Crown Press, 1955), p. 18.

21. Downie, *Swift, Political Writer*, p. 319. For a good brief essay on Swift's inverted seriousness see W. H. Irwin, "Swift the Verse Man," *Philological Quarterly* 54(1975): 222–38. See too Robert Uphaus, "Swift's Poetry: The Making of Meaning," *Eighteenth-Century Studies* 5(1971–72):585 and Jaffe, p. 59.

22. For a convenient summary see Arthur Scouten and Robert D. Hume, "Pope and Swift: Text and Interpretation of Swift's Verses on his Death," *Philological Quarterly* 52(1973): 205–31. For two excellent recent discussions see C. J. Rawson, "I the Lofty Stile Decline: Self-Apology and the 'heroick Strain' in some of Swift's Poems," in *The English Hero, 1660–1800*, ed. Robert Folkenflik (Newark: University of Delaware Press, 1982), pp. 101–2 and Richard Feingold, "Swift in his Poems," in *The Character of Swift's Satire, A Revised Focus*, ed. C. J. Rawson (London: Associated University Presses, 1983), pp. 166–202.

Chapter 8. "To Form the Manners": Pope and the Poetry of Mores

1. Satire 2. 1. 133, Butt, p. 618; for Pope's ideological purposes see Ellen Pollak, *The Poetics of Sexual Myth* and Laura Brown, *Alexander Pope* (Oxford: Basil Blackwell, 1985). According to Nora Crow Jaffe in a review of Laura Brown in *Eighteenth-Century Studies* 20(1986–87):248, Donald Patey spoke about Pope's ideological readjustment of old and new in *The Rape of the Lock* in a talk at Harvard in March 1986. References in the text to Pope are to *The Poems of Alexander Pope*, ed. John Butt (London: Methuen, 1963), except for notes 9 and 26, which cite a further edition.

2. Spence, *Observations*, ed. Osborn, 1, 244–45.

3. Spence, 1, 227–28.

4. *Correspondence* 2:182; "Imitations of Horace, Satire 2.2" 177–78, p. 624.

5. J. W. Johnston, *The Poet and the City: A Study in Urban Perspectives* (Athens, Ga.: University of Georgia Press, 1985), p. 41ff. See also Leopold Damrosch, Jr., *The Imaginative World of Alexander Pope* (Berkeley and Guildford: California University Press, 1987) p. 76.

6. *Poems* 9, ed. Mack, 4–5 and 42; "Preface to Shakespeare," *The Literary Criticism of Alexander Pope*, ed. Bertrand Goldgar (Lincoln, Nebr.: University of Nebraska Press, 1965), p. 164. For a study of Pope as court poet manqué see Ian Jack, "Pope and his Audience from 'The Pastorals' to the 'The Dunciad Variorum,'" *Studies in the Eighteenth Century* IV ed. R. F. Brissenden and J. C. Eade (Canberra, 1979), pp. 1–30.

7. G. S. Rousseau, "The Proper Study of Pope," *Times Literary Supplement*, 18 January 1980, p. 69.

8. *Correspondence* 2:227.

9. *Correspondence* 1:465.

10. *Correspondence* 1:109–10; Spence, 1:201.

11. Butt, p. xxviii.

12. Bertrand Bronson, *Man versus Society in Eighteenth-Century England*, ed. James Clifford (Cambridge: University Press, 1968), pp. 110–11. For other important studies see M. J. C. Hodgart, "The Subscription List for Pope's 'Iliad,'" "in *The Dress of Words: Essays on Restoration and Eighteenth-Century Literature in Honor of R. P. Bond*, ed. Robert B. White (Lawrence: University of Kansas Press, 1978), pp. 23–35; W. A. Speck, "Politicians, Peers and Publication by Subscription, 1700–1750," in *Books and their Readers in Eighteenth-Century England*, ed. Isobel Rivers (Leicester: University of Leicester Press, 1982); Pat Rogers, "Pope and his Subscribers," *Publishing History* 3(1978): 7–36.

13. Spence, 1:32.

14. "Essay on Criticism," 362–63, p. 155; Rawson, "Gentlemen and Dancing Masters," art. cit.

15. R. Kraft, "Class Analysis of a Literary Controversy: Wit and Sense in Seventeenth-Century English Literature," *Science and Society* 10(1946):80–92; E. N. Hooker, "Pope on Wit," in *Eighteenth-Century English Literature*, ed. James Clifford (New York: Oxford University Press, 1959), pp. 42–61.

16. See for example C. E. Nicholson, "A World of Artefacts: 'The Rape of the Lock' as Social History," *Literature and History* 5(1979): 189.

17. Pollak, *Poetics of Sexual Myth*, p. 180.

18. Brean Hammond, *Pope*, chap. 5, pp. 150–194.

19. See Piper, *Heroic Couplet*, pp. 139–43. Stephen Copley also made some valuable comments on this in a lecture at Reading in 1985.

20. Rawson, *Gulliver and the Gentle Reader* (London: Routledge and Kegan Paul, 1973), p. 54.

21. Doody, *Scriblerian* 19(1987): 180.

22. Rawson, *Order*, p. 255.

23. Richard Feingold, *Nature and Society: Later Eighteenth-Century Uses of the Pastoral and Georgic* (Brighton: Harvester, 1978), pp. 36–37.

24. Feingold, *Nature and Society*, p. 40.

25. *Correspondence* 3:52.

26. *Correspondence* 2:370; and postscript to *Odyssey* in *Poems* 9, ed. Mack, 389. *Poems*,

27. "Couplets on Wit," p. 295.

28. The idea of Pope's lack of "high seriousness" is, of course, Matthew Arnold's in "The Study of Poetry," *Essays in Criticism*, 2d ser.(1888).

29. *Correspondence* 4:377.

30. Bolingbroke, *Works* 1:502. I owe this reference to p. 74 of D. J. Hudson's Ph.D. thesis, "Pope, Bolingbroke and The *Craftsman* p. 74, cited previously.

31. *Correspondence* 4:342.

32. For an account of this trend see Trickett, *Honest Muse*, op. cit.

33. Thomas R. Edwards, "Heroic Folly: Pope's Satiric Identity," in *Pope: Recent Essays by Several Hands*, ed. Maynard Mack and James Winn (Brighton: Harvester Press, 1980), p. 579.

34. See 22, chapt. 7.

35. Paul Gabriner, "Pope's 'Virtue' and the Events of 1738," in *Pope: Recent Essays*, ed. Mack and Winn, pp. 585–611.

36. Aubrey Williams, *The Dunciad, A Study of its Meaning* (Baton Rouge: Louisiana State University Press, 1955).

Select Bibliography

Primary Materials

MAJOR EDITIONS USED

Gay, John. *Dramatic Works of John Gay.* Edited by John Fuller. 2 vols. Oxford: Clarendon Press, 1983.

———. *Letters of John Gay.* Edited by C. F. Burgess. Oxford: Clarendon Press, 1966.

———. *Poetry and Prose of John Gay.* Edited by V. A. Dearing and C. Beckwith. 2 vols. Oxford: Clarendon Press, 1974.

Parnell, Thomas. *Collected Poems of Thomas Parnell.* Edited by Claude Rawson and F. P. Lock. Newark: University of Delaware Press, 1989.

Pope, Alexander. *The Correspondence of Alexander Pope.* Edited by George Sherburn. 5 vols. Oxford: Clarendon Press, 1956.

———. *Literary Criticism of Alexander Pope.* Edited by Bertrand A. Goldgar. Lincoln: University of Nebraska Press, 1965.

———. *The Poems of Alexander Pope.* Edited by John Butt. London: Methuen, 1963.

———. *The Twickenham Edition of the Poems of Alexander Pope.* Edited by John Butt et al. 11 vols. New Haven: Yale University Press, 1939–69.

Prior, Matthew. *Literary Works of Matthew Prior.* Monroe K. Spears and George Bunker Wright. 2 vols. Oxford: Clarendon Press, 1959.

Swift, Jonathan. *Swift: Poetical Works.* Edited by Herbert Davis. Oxford: Clarendon Press, 1967.

———. *Prose Works of Jonathan Swift.* Edited by Herbert Davis. 14 vols. Oxford: Blackwell, 1939–68.

HISTORICAL AND LITERARY SOURCES

Addison, Joseph and Richard Steele. *The Guardian.* Edited by John Calhoun Stephens. Lexington: University of Kentucky Press, 1983.

———. *The Spectator.* Edited by D. F. Bond. 5 vols. Oxford: Clarendon Press, 1965.

———. *The Tatler.* Edited by D. F. Bond. 3 vols. Oxford: Clarendon Press, 1987.

Bolingbroke, Henry St. John, Viscount. *Works of Henry St. John, Viscount Bolingbroke.* 4 vols. 1841. Reprint. Philadelphia. Carey and Greg, 1969.

Castiglione, Baldassar. *The Book of the Courtier.* Translated by Hoby. London: Dent, 1928.

Chalmers, Alexander, ed. *Works of the English Poets*. 21 vols. London: J. Johnson, 1810.

Chaucer, Geoffrey. *Works of Geoffrey Chaucer*. Edited by F. N. Robinson. Cambridge, Mass.: Riverside Press, 1961.

Chesterfield, Philip Dormer Stanhope, Fourth Earl. *Letters of Philip Dormer Stanhope, Fourth Earl of Chesterfield*. Edited by Bonamy Dobrée. 1932. Reprint (6 vols.). New York: A. M. S. Press, 1966.

Collier, Jeremy. *A Short View of the Immorality and Profaneness of the English Stage*. London: S. Keble, 1698.

Copley, Stephen, ed. *Literature and the Social Order in Eighteenth-Century England*. Beckenham: Croom Helm, 1984.

Davenant, William. *Gondibert*. Edited by David F. Gladish. Oxford: Clarendon Press, 1971.

Defoe, Daniel. *Moll Flanders*. Edited by G. A. Starr. London: Oxford University Press, 1971.

Dennis, John. *Critical Works*. 2 vols. Edited by E. N. Hooker. Baltimore: Johns Hopkins University Press, 1939.

Donne, John. *John Donne: The Satires, Epigrams and Verse Letters*. Edited by W. Milgate. Oxford: Clarendon Press, 1967.

Dodsley, Robert. *Collection of Poems by Several Hands*. 3 vols. 2d ed. London: 1748.

Dryden, John. *Poems of John Dryden*. Edited by James Kinsley. 4 vols. Oxford: Clarendon Press, 1958.

Fielding, Henry. *Joseph Andrews*. Edited by Martin Battestin. Oxford: Clarendon Press, 1967.

Hume, David. *Hume's Essays Moral, Political and Literary*. Edited by T. Green and T. Grose. 2 vols. London: Longman's, 1898.

Jonson, Ben. *Works of Ben Jonson*. 11 vols. Edited by C. H. Herford and P. Simpson. Oxford: Clarendon Press, 1925–52.

Miege, Guy. "The Present State of Great Britain." In *Aristocratic Government and Society in Eighteenth-Century England*, edited by Daniel Baugh. New York: Franklin Watts, 1975.

Peake, Charles, ed. *Poetry of the Landscape and the Night*. London: Edward Arnold, 1967.

Pervigilium Veneris. In *Catullus, Tibullus and Pervigilium Veneris*, edited by F. W. Cornish, J. P. Postgate, and J. W. Mackail. Cambridge: Harvard University Press, 1962.

Rochester, John WIlmot, Earl of. *The Poems of John Wilmot, Earl of Rochester*. Edited by Keith Walker. Oxford: Blackwell, 1984.

Ryder, Dudley. *Diary*. Edited by William Matthews. London: Methuen, 1968.

Shaftesbury, Third Earl of, *Characteristics of Men, Manners, Opinions Times*. Edited by M. Robertson. Indianapolis: Bobbs-Merril, 1964.

Smith, Sir Thomas. *De Republica Anglorum*. Edited by L. Alston. Cambridge: University Press, 1906.

Spence, Joseph. *Observations, Anecdotes and Characters of Books and Men*. Edited by James Osborn. 2 vols. Oxford: Clarendon Press, 1966.

Spenser, Edmund. *The Fairie Queene*. Edited by A. C. Hamilton. London: Longmans, 1977.

Spingarn, J. E., ed. *Critical Essays of the Seventeenth Century*. 3 vols. 1908–9. Reprint. Bloomington: University of Indiana Press, 1957.

Thomson, James. *Letters and Documents*. Edited by A. D. McKillop. Lawrence: University of Kansas Press, 1958.

———. *Liberty, The Castle of Indolence and Other Poems*. Edited by James Sambrook. Oxford: Clarendon Press, 1986.

———. *The Seasons*. Edited by James Sambrook. Oxford: Clarendon Press, 1981.

Waller, Edmund. *Poems of Edmund Waller*. 2 vols. Edited by G. B. Thorn Drury. London: Routledge, 1905.

Winchelsea, Anne Finch, Countess of. *Poems of Anne Finch, Countess of Winchelsea*. Edited by Myra Reynolds. Chicago: University of Chicago Press, 1903.

Secondary Sources

HISTORICAL AND SOCIAL STUDIES

Baugh, Daniel, ed. *Aristocratic Government and Society in Eighteenth-Century England*. New York: Franklin Watts, 1975.

Bourdieu, Pierre. *Outline of a Theory of Practice*. Translated by R. Nice. Cambridge: University Press, 1977.

Brauer, George A., Jr. "Good Breeding in the Eighteenth Century." *University of Texas Studies in English* 32(1953):25–44.

Cannon, John. *Aristocratic Century: The Peerage of Eighteenth-Century England*. Cambridge: University Press, 1984.

Castronovo, David. *The English Gentleman: Image and Ideals in Literature and Society*. New York: Ungar, 1987.

Clark, Alice. *Working Life of Women in the Seventeenth Century*. London: Routledge, 1919.

Clark, J. C. D. *English Society, 1688–1832: Ideology, Social Structure and Political Practice during the Ancien Régime*. Cambridge: University Press, 1985.

Curtis, T. A. and W. A. Speck. "The Societies for the Reformation of Manners: A Case History in the Theory and Practice of Moral Reform." *Literature and History* 3(1976): 45–64.

Davidoff, Leonore. *The Best Circles*. London: Cresset Books, 1986.

Dickson, P. M. G. *The Financial Revolution in England: A Study in the Development of Public Credit 1688–1756*. London: Macmillan, 1967.

Elias, Norbert. *The Civilising Process*. Oxford: Basil Blackwell, 1978.

———. *State Formation and Civilisation*. Oxford: Blackwell, 1981.

Everitt, Alan. "Social Mobility in Early Modern England." *Past and Present* 33 (1966): 56–73.

Foss, Michael. *The Age of Patronage: The Arts in Society, 1660–1750*. London: Hamish Hamilton, 1971.

Furbank, P. N. *Unholy Pleasure: The Idea of Social Class.* Oxford: University Press, 1985.

Goldie, Mark. "The Rise of Politeness." Review of *Virtue, Commerce and History* by J. G. A. Pocock. *Times Literary Supplement,* 27 June 1986, p. 715.

Greenleaf, W. H. *Order, Empiricism and Politics: Two Traditions of English Political Thought, 1500–1700.* Oxford: University Press, 1964.

Hammond, Mason. *The City in the Ancient World.* Cambridge: Harvard University Press, 1972.

Hanson, Donald. *From Kingdom to Commonwealth: The Development of Civic Consciousness in English Political Thought.* Cambridge: Harvard University Press, 1970.

Jacob, Margaret C. *The Newtonians and the English Constitution, 1689–1720.* Hassocks, Sussex: Harvester, 1976.

Jarrett, Derek. *England in the Age of Hogarth.* London: Hart-Davis, MacGibbon, 1974.

Keen, Maurice. *Chivalry.* New Haven: Yale University Press, 1984.

Kelso, Ruth. *The Doctrine of the English Gentleman in the Sixteenth Century.* Urbana: University of Illinois Press, 1929.

Klein, Lawrence. "The Third Earl of Shaftesbury and the Progress of Politeness." *Eighteenth-Century Studies* 18(1984–85): 186–214.

Kramnick, Isaac. *Bolingbroke and his Circle: the Politics of Nostalgia in the Age of Walpole.* Cambridge: Harvard University Press, 1968.

Lévi-Strauss, Claude. *Tristes Tropiques.* Translated by John Russell. New York: Criterion Books, 1961.

Macintyre, Alasdair. *After Virtue: A Study in Moral Theory.* London: Duckworth, 1981.

McKendrick, Neil, John Brewer, and J. H. Plumb. *The Birth of a Consumer Society: The Commercialization of Eighteenth-Century England.* London: Hutchinson, 1984.

McLellan, David. *Ideology.* Milton Keynes: Open University Press, 1987.

Magendie, Maurice. *La Politesse Mondaine et les Théories de l'honnêteté en France, au XVIIe Siècle de 1600–1660.* 2 vols. Paris: Alcan, 1926.

Malcolmson, R. W. *Popular Recreations in English Society, 1700–1850.* Cambridge: University Press, 1973.

Mason, John. *Gentlefolk in the Making: Studies in the History of English Courtesy Literature and Related Topics from 1531–1774.* Philadelphia: University of Pennsylvania Press, 1953.

Morrall, John B. *The Medieval Imprint.* Harmondsworth: Penguin Books, 170.

Neale, R. S. *Class in English History, 1600–1850.* Oxford: Blackwell, 1981.

Newman, Gerald. *The Rise of English Nationalism: A Cultural History 1740–1830.* London: Weidenfeld and Nicolson, 1987.

Nicholson, Harold. *Good Behaviour: Being a Study of Certain Types of Civility.* Boston: Beacon Press, 1960.

Plumb, J. H. *England in the Eighteenth Century.* Harmondsworth: Penguin 1968.

Pocock, J. G. A. *The Machiavellian Moment: Florentine Political Thought and* the *Atlantic Republican Tradition*. Princeton: Princeton University Press, 1977.

————. *Virtue, Commerce and History: Essays on Political Thought and History, Chiefly in the Eighteenth Century*. Cambridge: University Press, 1986.

Porter, Roy. *English Society in the Eighteenth Century*. The Pelican Social History of Britain. Harmondsworth: Pelican, 1982.

————. "The Enlightenment in England." In *The Enlightenment in National Context*, edited by Porter and M. Teich. Cambridge: University Press, 1981.

Rogers, Nicholas. "Money, Land and Lineage: The Big Bourgeoisie of Hanoverian London." *Social History* 4(1979): 437–54.

Rudé, George. *Hanoverian London 1714–1818*. London: Secker and Warburg, 1971.

Sekora, John. *Luxury: The Concept in Western Thought, Eden to Smollett*. Baltimore: Johns Hopkins University Press, 1977.

Sennet, Richard. *The Fall of Public Man*. Cambridge: University Press, 1974.

Speck, W. A. *Stability and Strife: England 1714–1760*. London: Edward Arnold, 1977.

Stone, Lawrence. *The Family, Sex and Marriage in England, 1500–1800*. London: Weidenfeld and Nicolson, 1977.

————. *An Open Elite? England 1540–1880*. Oxford: Clarendon Press, 1984.

————. "Social Mobility in England, 1500–1700." *Past and Present* 33(1966): 16–55.

Thomas, P. W. "Two Cultures? Court and Country under Charles." In *The Origins of the English Civil War*, edited by Conrad Russell. London: Macmillan, 1973.

Thompson, E. P. "Eighteenth-century English Society: Class Struggle without Class?" *Social History* 3(1978): 133–65.

————. "Patrician Society, Plebeian Culture." *Journal of Social History* 7(1974): 382–405.

Veblen, Thorstein. *The Theory of the Leisure Class*. London: Allen and Unwin, 1925.

Vogt, George. "Gleanings of the History of a Sentiment." *Journal of English and Germanic Philology* 24(1925): 105–25.

Wildblood, Joan and Peter Brenson. *The Polite World*. London: Oxford University Press, 1965.

Williams, E. Neville. *Life in Georgian England*. London: Batsford, 1962.

Williams, Raymond. *Keywords: A Vocabulary of Culture and Society*. London: Croom Helm and Fontana, 1976.

LITERARY CRITICISM AND THEORY

Barrell, John. *The Dark Side of the Landscape*. Cambridge: University Press, 1980.

————. *An Equal Wide Survey, English Literature in History*. London: Hutchinson, 1983.

————. "Gainsborough's Rural Vision." *The Listener*, 12 May 1977, pp. 615–16.

Bate, Walter Jackson. *The Burden of the Past and the English Poet.* London: Chatto and Windus, 1971.

Bloom, Edward, Lillian D. Bloom, and Edward Leites. *Educating the Audience: Addison and Steele and Eighteenth-Century Culture.* Los Angeles: Clark Memorial Library, 1984.

Bredvold, Louis. "The Gloom of the Tory Satirists." In *Eighteenth-Century English Literature: Modern Essays in Criticism,* edited by James L. Clifford, pp. 3–20. New York: Oxford University Press, 1959.

Brewer, D. S. "Class Distinction in Chaucer." *Speculum* 43(1968): 290–305.

Bronson, Bertrand. *Man versus Society in Eighteenth-Century England.* Edited by James Clifford. Cambridge: University Press, 1968.

Brower, Reuben. "Dryden and the Invention of Pope." In *Restoration and Eighteenth-Century Literature: Essays in Honour of A. D. Mckillop,* pp. 211–34. Chicago: University of Chicago Press, 1963.

Brown, Laura. *Alexander Pope: Rereading Literature.* Oxford: Basil Blackwell, 1985.

Brown, Marshall. "The Urbane Sublime," *ELH* 45 (1978): 236–54.

Butler, Martin. *Theatre and Crisis 1632–1642.* Cambridge: University Press, 1984.

Chaffin, C. E. "The Two Cities: Christian and Pagan Literary Styles in Rome." In *The Classical World,* edited by David Daiches and Anthony Thorlby. London: Aldus Books, 1972, pp. 461–86.

Chapin, Chester. *Personification in English Poetry.* New York: Kings Crown Press, 1955.

Chernaik, W. L. "The Heroic Occasional Peom: Panegyric and Satire in the Restoration." *Modern Language Quarterly* 26(1965): 523–35.

———. *The Poetry of Limitation: A Study of Edmund Waller.* New Haven: Yale University Press, 1968.

Cohen, Ralph. *The Unfolding of "The Seasons".* London: Routledge and Kegan Paul, 1970.

Collins, A. S. "The Growth of the Reading Public during the Eighteenth Century." *Review of English Studies* 2(1926): 284–93; 428–38.

Copley, Stephen. "Luxury, Refuse and Poetry: John Gay's "Trivia." In *Gay and the Scriblerians,* edited by Nigel Wood and Peter Lewis. London: Vision Press, 1988; New York: St. Martin's Press, 1989.

Courthope, W. J. *A History of English Poetry.* 6 vols. London: Macmillan, 1895–1910.

Damrosch, Leopold, Jr. *The Imaginative World of Alexander Pope.* Berkeley and Guildford: California University Press, 1987.

Dircks, Richard. "Parnell's 'Batrachomuomachia' and the Homer Translation Controversy." *Notes and Queries* 201(1956): 339–42.

Dixon, Peter. *The World of Pope's Satires.* London: Methuen, 1968.

Dobrée, Bonamy. "The Theme of Patriotism in Poetry of the Early Eighteenth Century, 1700–1740." *Proceedings of the British Academy* 35(1949): 49–65.

Doody, Margaret. Review of *Alexander Pope* by Laura Brown. *The Scriblerian* 19(1987): 179–80.

Downie, J. A. *Jonathan Swift, Political Writer.* London: Routledge and Kegan Paul, 1984.

———. Review of *Swift's Tory Politics* by F. P. Lock. *Eighteenth-Century Studies* 19 (1985): 113–15.

Draper, J. W. *The Funeral Elegy and the Rise of English Romanticism.* New York: New York University Press, 1929.

Eagleton, Terry. *The Function of Criticism: The Spectator to Post-Structuralism.* London: Verso, 1984.

———. *Literary Theory: An Introduction.* Oxford: Blackwell, 1983.

Edwards, Thomas R. "Heroic Folly: Pope's Satiric Identity." In *Pope: Recent Essays by Several Hands*, edited by Maynard Mack and James Winn, pp. 565–84. Brighton: Harvester Press, 1980.

Elioseff, Lee Andrew. "Joseph Addison's Political Animal." *Eighteenth-Century Studies* 6 (1973): 372–81.

Empson, William. *Some Versions of Pastoral.* London: Chatto and Windus, 1935.

Erskine-Hill, Howard. *The Augustan Idea in English Literature.* London: Edward Arnold, 1983.

———. *The Social Milieu of Alexander Pope: Lives, Example and the Poetic Response.* New Haven: Yale University Press, 1975.

Fairchild, H. N. *Religious Trends in English Poetry.* Vol. 1. New York: Columbia University Press, 1939.

Feingold, Richard. *Nature and Society: Later Eighteenth-Century Uses of the Pastoral and Georgic.* Brighton: Harvester, 1978.

———. "Swift in his Poems." In *The Character of Swift's Satire: A Revised Focus*, edited by C. J. Rawson, pp. 166–202. Newark, Del.: University of Delaware Press, 1983.

Fineman, Daniel A. "Leonard Welsted: Gentleman Poet of the Augustan Age." Ph.D. dissertation, University of Philadelphia, 1950.

Robert Folkenflik, "Patronage and the Poet-Hero," *Huntingdon Library Quarterly* 48 (1985): 363–79.

Gabriner, Paul. "Pope's 'Virtue' and the Events of 1738." In *Pope: Recent Essays*, edited by Maynard Mack and James Winn, pp. 585–611. Brighton: Harvester Press, 1980.

Gilmour, Robin. *The Idea of the Gentleman in the Victorian Novel.* London: Allen and Unwin, 1981.

Goldgar, Bertrand A. *Walpole and the Wits: The Relation of Politics to Literature, 1722–1742.* Lincoln, Nebr.: University of Nebraska Press, 1976.

Gosse, Edmund. *A History of Eighteenth-Century English Literature.* London: Macmillan, 1889.

Graham, Edwin. "John Gay's Second Series: The Craftsman in the Fables." *Papers in Language and Literature* (1969): 17–25.

Guilhamet, Leon. *The Sincere Ideal: Studies in Sincerity in Eighteenth-Century Literature.* Montreal and London: McGill-Queens University Press, 1974.

Hall, Basil. "An Inverted Hypocrite: Swift the Churchman." In *The World of Jonathan Swift*, edited by Brian Vickers, pp. 36–68. Oxford: Basil Blackwell, 1968.

Hammond, Brean. "'A Poet and a Patron and Ten Pound': Patronage in Gay's Poetry." In *Gay and the Scriblerians*, edited by Nigel Wood and Peter Lewis. London: Vision Press, 1988; New York: St. Martin's Press, 1989.

————. *Pope*. Brighton: Harvester Press, 1986.

Havens, R. D. "Parnell's 'Hymn to Contentment.'" *Modern Language Notes* 59(1944): 329–31.

Helgerson, Richard. *Self-Crowned Laureates: Spenser, Jonson, Milton and the Literary System*. Berkeley and Los Angeles: University of California Press, 1983.

Heltzel, V. B. "Chesterfield and the Tradition of the Ideal Gentleman." Ph.D. dissertation, University of Chicago, 1925.

Hodgart, M. J. C. "The Subscription List for Pope's 'Iliad,'" In *The Dress of Words: Essays on Restoration and Eighteenth-Century Literature in Honor of R. P. Bond*, edited by Robert B. White, pp. 23–35. Lawrence: University of Kansas Press, 1978.

Hooker, E. N. "Pope on Wit: The *Essay on Criticism*." In *Eighteenth-Century English Literature*, edited by James Clifford pp. 42–61. New York: Oxford University Press, 1959.

Hudson, A. P. "The Hermit and Divine Providence." *Studies in Philology* 28 (1931): 218–34.

Hudson, D. J. "Pope, Bolingbroke and *The Craftsman*." Ph.D. dissertation, University of Reading, 1978.

Hume, Anthea. *Edmund Spenser, Protestant Poet*. Cambridge: University Press, 1984.

Irwin, W. H. "Swift the Verse Man." *Philological Quarterly* 54 (1975): 222–238.

Jack, Ian. "Pope and his Audience from 'The Pastorals' to the 'The Dunciad Variorum.'" *Studies in the Eighteenth Century* IV ed. R. F. Brissenden and J. C. Eade. Canberra: Australian University Press, 1979, pp. 1–30.

Jaffe, Nora Crow. *The Poet Swift*. Hanover, N.H.: University of New England Press, 1977.

Javitch, Daniel. *Poetry and Courtliness in Renaissance England*. Princeton: Princeton University Press, 1978.

Johnston, J. W. *The Poet and the City: A Study in Urban Perspectives*. Athens, Ga.: University of Georgia Press, 1985.

Kernan, Alvin. *The Plot of Satire*. New Haven: Yale University Press, 1965.

Kraft, R. "Class Analysis of a Literary Controversy: Wit and Sense in Seventeenth-Century English Literature." *Science and Society* 10 (1946): 80–89.

Landre, Louis. *Leigh Hunt*. Paris: Editions Belles Lettres, 1936.

Lee, Jae Num. *Swift and Scatological Satire*. Albuquerque: University of New Mexico Press, 1971.

Lock, F. P. *Swift's Tory Politics*. London: Duckworth, 1983.

McKeon, Michael. *The Origins of the English Novel, 1600–1740.* London and Baltimore: Johns Hopkins University Press, 1987.

Manley, Lawrence. *Convention, 1500–1750*. Cambridge: Harvard University Press, 1980.

Marks, Sylvia Kasey. "*Sir Charles Grandison*," *The Complete Conduct Book*. Lewisburg, Pa.: Bucknell University Press, 1986.

Moore, C. A. "Whig Panegyric Verse, 1700–1760." *PMLA* 41 (1926): 362–401.

Morris, David. *Alexander Pope, Genius of Sense*. Cambridge: Harvard University Press, 1984.

———. *The Religious Sublime.* Lexington: Kentucky University Press, 1972.

Nicholson, C. E. "A World of Artefacts: 'The Rape of the Lock' as Social History," *Literature and History* 5 (1979):183–93.

Nussbaum, Felicity A. *The Brink of All We Hate: English Satires on Women, 1660–1750.* Lexington: University of Kentucky Press, 1984.

Parrinder, Patrick. *The Failure of Theory: Essays on Criticism of Contemporary Fiction.* Brighton: Harvester, 1987.

Patterson, Annabel M. *Marvell and the Civic Crown.* Princeton: Princeton University Press, 1978.

Paulson, Ronald. *Popular and Polite Art in the Age of Hogarth and Fielding.* London and Notre Dame: University of Notre Dame Press, 1979.

Piper, W. B. *The Heroic Couplet.* Cleveland: Case Western Reserve University Press, 1969.

Pollak, Ellen. *The Poetics of Sexual Myth: Gender and Ideology in the Verse of Swift and Pope.* Chicago: University of Chicago Press, 1985.

Ramage, Edwin S. *Urbanitas: Ancient Sophistication and Refinement.* Norman: University of Oklahoma Press, 1973.

Rawson, C. J. "Gentlemen and Dancing Masters: Thoughts on Fielding, Chesterfield and the Genteel." *Eighteenth-Century Studies* 1(1967–68): 127–58.

———. *Gulliver and the Gentle Reader.* London: Routledge and Kegan Paul, 1973.

———. *Henry Fielding and the Augustan Ideal under Stress.* London: Routledge and Kegan Paul, 1972.

———. "I the Lofty Stile Decline: Self-Apology and the 'Heroick Strain' in Some of Swift's Poems." In *The English Hero, 1660–1800,* edited by Robert Folkenflik, pp. 79–115. Newark: University of Delaware Press, 1982.

———. "New Parnell Manuscripts." *Scriberlian* 1(1969): 1–2.

———. *Order from Confusion Sprung: Studies in Eighteenth-Century Literature from Swift to Cowper.* London: Allen and Unwin, 1985.

———. "Swift's Certificate to Parnell's 'Posthumous Works.'" *Modern Language Review* 57 (1962): 179–82.

Rees, Christine. "Gay, Swift and the Nymphs of Drury Lane." *Essays in Criticism* 23(1973): 1–21.

Rippy, Frances M. *Matthew Prior.* Boston: Twayne, 1986.

———. "Matthew Prior and Alexander Pope: Their Personal and Literary Relationship." Ph.D. dissertation, Vanderbilt University, 1957.

Robinson, Alan. "Swift and Renaissance Poetry: A Declaration of Independence." *British Journal for Eighteenth-Century Studies* 8 (1985): 37–49.

Rogers, Katharine M. *The Troublesome Helpmate: A History of Misogyny in Literature.* Seattle: University of Washington Press, 1966.

Rogers, Pat. "Pope and his Subscribers." *Publishing History* 3(1978): 7–36.

———, ed. *The Eighteenth Century.* London: Methuen, 1978.

Rousseau, G. S. "The Proper Study of Pope." *Times Literary Supplement,* 18 January 1980, p. 69.

Rower, Ronald. "Pastoral Wars: Prior's Poems to Chloe." *Ball State University Forum* 19(1978):38–49.

Saunders, J. W. "The Social Situation of Seventeenth Century Poetry." In *Metaphysical Poetry*. Stratford-upon-Avon Studies 2, edited by Malcolm Bradbury and John Palmer. London: Edward Arnold, 1970, pp. 237–59.

———. "The Stigma of Print." *Essays in Criticism* 1, (1959): 139–64.

Selden, Ramon. *English Verse Satire*. London: Allen and Unwin, 1978.

Shinagel, Michael. *Defoe and Middle-Class Gentility*. Cambridge: Harvard University Press, 1968.

Shrof, Homai. *The Eighteenth-Century Novel: The Idea of the Gentleman*. London: Edward Arnold, 1979.

Siebert, Donald T. "Swift's 'Fiat Odor:' The Excremental Re-vision." *Eighteenth-Century Studies* 19(1985): 21–38.

Solomon, Harry M. *Sir Richard Blackmore*. Boston: Twayne, 1980.

Spacks, Patricia. *John Gay*. New York: Twayne, 1965.

Spate, O. H. K. "The Muse of Mercantilism: Jago, Grainger and Dyer." In *Studies in the Eighteenth Century*, edited by R. F. Brissenden, pp. 119–31. Canberra: Australian National University Press, 1968.

Spears, Monroe K. "Ethical Aspects of Prior's Poetry." *Studies in Philology* 45(1948): 606–29.

———. "The Meaning of Prior's 'Alma.'" *English Literary History* 13(1946): 266–90.

Speck, W. L. "Politicians, Peers and Publication by Subscription, 1700–1750." In *Books and Their Readers in Eighteenth-Century England*, edited by Isabel Rivers, pp. 47–68. Leicester: University Press, 1982.

———. *Society and Literature in England, 1700–1760*. Dublin: Gill and Macmillan, 1983.

Stallybrass, Peter and Allon White. *The Politics and Poetics of Transgression*. London: Methuen, 1986.

Stanton, Domna. *The Aristocrat as Art: A Study of the Honnête Homme and the Dandy in Seventeenth- and Nineteenth-Century French Literature*. New York: Columbia University Press, 1980.

Steensma, Robert. *Dr. John Arbuthnot*. Boston: Twayne, 1979.

Sutherland, James. *A Preface to Eighteenth-Century Poetry*. London: Oxford University Press, 1963.

Tonkin, Humphrey. *Spenser's Courteous Pastoral*. Oxford: Clarendon Press, 1972.

Trickett, Rachel. *The Honest Muse: A Study in Augustan Verse*. Oxford: Clarendon Press, 1967.

Trilling, Lionel. *Sincerity and Authenticity*. London: Oxford University Press, 1972.

Uphaus, Robert. "Swift's Poetry: The Making of Meaning." *Eighteenth-Century Studies* 5 (1971–72): 569–86.

Warren, Austin. *Rage for Order*. Chicago: University of Chicago Press, 1948.

Wayne, Don E. *Penhurst: The Semiotics of Place and the Poetics of History*. London: Methuen, 1984.

Weinbrot, Howard. *Augustus Caesar in "Augustan" England*. Princeton: Princeton University Press, 1978.

Williams, Aubrey. *The Dunciad: A Study of Its Meaning*. Baton Rouge: Louisiana State University Press, 1955.

Womack, Peter. *Ben Jonson: Rereading Literature*. Oxford: Blackwell, 1987.

Woodman, Thomas. "Parnell, Politeness and Pre-Romanticism," *Essays in Criticism* 33 (1983): 205–19.

———. "Pope and the Polite," *Essays in Criticism* 28 (1978): 19–37.

———. *Thomas Parnell*. Boston: Twayne, 1985.

———. " 'Vulgar Circumstance' and 'Due Civilities:' John Gay's Art of Polite Living in Town." In *Gay and the Scriblerians*, edited by Nigel Wood and Peter Lewis. London: Vision Press, 1988; New York: St. Martin's Press, 1989.

Woolf, Virginia. *The Common Reader*. 2d ser. London: Hogarth Press, 1935.

Index